DAUGHTERS OF ERIN

Five Women
Of the Irish Renascence

Elizabeth Coxhead

COLIN SMYTHE
Gerrards Cross, 1979

Copyright © 1965 by Elizabeth Coxhead

First published in 1965
First paperback edition published in 1979
by Colin Smythe Limited, Gerrards Cross, Buckinghamshire

Distributed in N. America by Humanities Press Inc.,
171 First Avenue, Atlantic Highlands, N.J. 07716

British Library Cataloguing in Publication Data

Coxhead, Elizabeth
    Daughters of Erin.
    1. Women – Ireland – Biography
    I. Title
    920.72′09415   CT3650.I/

    ISBN 0–901072–60–5

Printed in Great Britain
by Billing & Sons Ltd., Guildford, London & Worcester

DAUGHTERS OF ERIN

CONTENTS

ILLUSTRATIONS

AUTHOR'S NOTE

MY PRINCIPAL sources are given at the end of each section, and I am deeply grateful to all those listed therein, who helped me with their reminiscences or material.

Quotations from the poems of W. B. Yeats are by permission of Michael B. Yeats and Anne Yeats and Messrs. Macmillan & Co., from the poems and letters of J. M. Synge by permission of Dr. Ann Saddlemyer and the Oxford University Press, from *Prison Letters of Countess Markievicz* by permission of Sir Paul Gore-Booth and Messrs. Longmans, Green & Co.

I owe my illustrations to Mrs. Sean MacBride, Lady Gore-Booth, Professor John Purser, Professor D. J. Gordon, Bord Fáilte Eireann, the National Library of Ireland, and the British Lion Film Corporation.

E. C.

DAUGHTERS OF ERIN

INTRODUCTION

IRELAND, more than most, is a man's country, and for all the feminine grace of its streets and setting, Dublin is a man's town. The famous talk is largely masculine talk; the new ideas are sparked off in clubs and bars which are still largely a male preserve. Women sit in the Dail, it is true, but usually widows or descendants of noted patriots. Now and again the newspapers deplore the small part taken by women in public life, and thereby provoke tart letters from wives and mothers pointing out how little encouragement they are given— debarred as they are by marriage from the Civil Service, from paid posts in local government, and from other influential occupations.

This is the reaction of the clever and the ambitious; the majority, diffident and apathetic, seem to have acquiesced. The often excessive mother-cult of which they are the object gives them, at best, a backstairs influence. The lot of the younger is not made easier by the fact that so many of their potential husbands emigrate. One pretty Dublin girl after another will tell you the same story: "Here, the boys are kings."

Perhaps it was always so; certainly Irish history seems to be masculine history until we get back to the legendary Queen Maeve. But there is one exception—the cardinal episode which liberated the country from English rule. In the Irish Renascence, political, literary and artistic (for it was all part of the same impulse) women played a vital part, fought, plotted, planned, wrote, painted, acted, alongside their male comrades as equals, and while most of these comrades

13

were languishing in English gaols, kept the revolutionary spirit alive.

And then, when victory was won, they were thanked and sent back to the domestic hearth. Those who made nuisances of themselves in protest were visited with the utmost opprobrium and resentment, traces of which persist. The rest are forgotten.

Lady Gregory was one of the two key figures in the literary revival, though her part in it has been but grudgingly acknowledged, as I have observed elsewhere. The political leaders, Maud Gonne and Constance Markievicz, were backed by a host of heroines, most of them unsung. Without Sarah Purser, the stained glass which is the movement's chief glory on the artistic side could never have been created. And the new drama, though it had many gifted male interpreters, looked to its two leading ladies for the quality of magic which gave it a hold on audiences far beyond Irish shores.

There are many others who might well have figured in what one of my Dublin acquaintances rather unkindly called "your female Valhalla". Kathleen Lynn, for example, the doctor of the Easter Rising, and founder of the hospital which has saved thousands of infant lives. Susan Mitchell, the wit (but it is impossible to disentangle her from the shadow of her mentor George Russell). Katharine Tynan, the poet and friend of poets (but half her career was spent out of Ireland). Mrs. Despard, the viceroy's sister turned red revolutionary. Hannah Sheehy-Skeffington, the suffragette leader who had probably the best brain of them all.

But I have chosen the five whose strongly contrasted characters and achievements most nearly correspond (or so it seems to me) to what was going on in the violent and complicated times through which they lived. All knew each other, their paths sometimes crossing dramatically; for it is one of the great merits of Dublin that people do know each other, are not lost in suburban backwaters as they are in

London, but are for ever getting in each other's way, with a consequent continual quarrelsome, revivifying clash of temperaments and ideas.

All but one were wives and mothers, and thus may be held to have fulfilled Nature's purpose; and the spinster was so active at the heart of a large and close-knit clan that she can fairly be considered a family woman too. And two of them inspired the best work of great writers, an honour which is apt to bring with it the drawback of considerable posthumous distortion and abuse.

But the important factor they have in common is a devotion to something bigger than themselves and their immediate circles. One could call it Ireland, but Ireland in different guises. The two political women were passionate champions of Irish freedom, which they equated with the cause of the poor and the oppressed. The painter and the actresses gave of their best to others' art as well as their own.

Without something of the capacity to transcend the confines of private life, no one, man or woman, can be considered a complete human being. This is essentially the story of five women's struggles—struggles made fiercer by Victorian and Edwardian convention, by every sort of difficulty and discouragement—to live the lives of complete human beings in a man's world.

Maud Gonne

I

OF ALL the beauties that have inspired great poetry, hers is perhaps the best vouched for by contemporaries. A poet's word is not to be taken for it; of course his Muse must excel. But even those who did not like Maud Gonne, even those who found her personality antipathetic and her politics disastrous, never disputed her amazing looks. There are many still living who can remember her startlingly handsome in middle age; and I have talked with several (Geoffrey Winthrop Young, for instance, in the last year of his life) who remembered her prime. The verdict is always the same: "The most beautiful person I ever saw."

She was very tall, nearly six feet, with masses of auburn hair, and strange golden eyes. "A natural born queen, Helen of Troy," says Helena Molony, who recalls the fun of walking behind her through the Dublin streets just to watch the effect she had on passers-by. Business-men, deep in discussion of share prices, would break off their talk to gape at this vision, this being from another world. . . .

"Her extraordinary beauty drew all eyes to her," writes Katharine Tynan in her memoirs. "In keeping with her beauty was an exquisite voice. She dressed beautifully as well, and in Dublin, where taste is not a strong point, her dress made her as conspicuous as her beauty. When one met her walking in a Dublin street one felt as if a goddess had come to earth."

Physical perfection alone could not have done it. She had also the glamour of the dedicated being; she was Kathleen ni Houlihan, personification of the Irish cause. Yet she combined her aura of *princesse lointaine* with a warmth and winning friendliness not commonly associated with symbols. Here is Arthur Lynch, Paris correspondent of the *Daily Mail*. "When I knew Maud Gonne first she was at the height of her beauty, but the influence she exercised, though in part due to this, arose in a higher manner from her great qualities—courage, generosity and kindness. . . . Mr. Stead had met her in St. Petersburg, and he declared her to be the most beautiful woman in Europe. . . . She had a manner, not altogether an affectation, of looking at visitors, each one in turn, as if he or she were the one person on earth whom Miss Gonne had been longing to see."

Naturally, being young and fair, she had the wit to know it. Looking back in old age on the picture of herself and Yeats, "a tall lanky boy", sitting at the feet of old John O'Leary, she sees "a tall girl with masses of golden-brown hair and a beauty which made her Paris clothes unnoticeable". But it was something she regarded with detachment, a weapon to be used for Ireland, like everything else she possessed. "You know, it was rather a time of professional beauties," she told Thomas MacGreevy. "I'll let you know who was beautiful—a girl called Maud Guinness, who came out the year after I did. Yes, I think Maud Guinness was more beautiful than I was."

Yet Maud Guinness has left no legend. Maud Gonne will inevitably—literature having so much more staying-power than life—be remembered first of all as the inspiration of one who has been called the greatest modern love-poet. But for all the praise he lavished on her, he has given her to us in a distorting mirror. The heroic image, enshrined in so many simple hearts, may not have been at all points accurate either, but it was a great deal nearer to the truth.

Of recorded likeness, we retain very little. Her leonine fire was not to be captured by the photographer's lens of her youth; it presented merely a rather podgy, chocolate-box prettiness. The painter's brush should have done better, but old J. B. Yeats, the best Irish portraitist of the period, would only paint those with whom he was in sympathy, and naturally this did not include the young woman who persisted in breaking his son's heart. Sarah Purser tried twice, and in my opinion muffed both chances, but then Sarah was primarily a painter of intellectual, not sensuous, good looks. Only the Horvath photographs of extreme old age are in any sense magical.

But it does not signify. Beauty lives by impact, far more surely than by representation. We make our own image of Helen, and her mirror is burning Troy. We accept that Maud Gonne, "singing upon her road, half lion, half child", existed as a physical presence extraordinary, though not unique. She was the miracle that happens once in a generation, or perhaps once in a hundred years.

2

She was born in 1866 near Aldershot, where her father, an officer in the 17th Lancers, was stationed. The Gonnes claimed Mayo descent, but had been English for several generations and done well in the wine trade. Her mother, Edith Cook, was wholly English and also of a prosperous family. Grandfather Cook had made a notable collection of Old Masters, which should, Maud considered, have come to his only daughter, but instead were mysteriously appropriated by a great-uncle.

Lovely and consumptive, Edith Gonne died when Maud was four and her sister Kathleen two. Thomas Gonne did not remarry, but had his daughters brought up, first by a nurse in Ireland and then by a French governess on the Riviera, spending with them all the time his military duties allowed.

He treated them as companions and equals, and though Kathleen was diffident, Maud had the happy fearlessness often found in the motherless daughters of indulgent fathers. He was "Tommy" to her, in an age when most young ladies addressed their fathers as Papa or Sir.

Mademoiselle supplied the necessary element of rational discipline. She proved a much better teacher than the average governess, particularly of history. She was a strong republican, and her notions of equality and freedom fell, in Maud's case, on receptive ears.

In 1882 Colonel Gonne was posted as Assistant Adjutant-General to Dublin, and summoned the girls to join him. Maud had already received her first proposal—an unsuitable one, in the Colosseum, by moonlight—and he felt it was as well to have her under his eye. His friends advised him to engage a chaperone, but Maud at sixteen was confident that she could play the part of official hostess, and succeeded superbly. She was presented at the viceregal court, in an Art Nouveau dress with a train of stencilled water-lilies; she called on the officers' wives of every new regiment stationed in Dublin; she instituted regular afternoon teas for the generals, whose conversation she found more stimulating than that of the younger officers. She rode, she hunted, she was the Daughter of the Garrison to the life.

But beneath the surface in Land League Ireland were currents which Mademoiselle's pupil could not fail to detect. From the hunting landlords she heard of outrages, but the tones in which they spoke of their tenants, and their open rejoicing in evictions and other forms of reprisal, left her in no doubt where the real injustice lay. Watching a Land League procession march up to Phoenix Park to be addressed by Davitt and Dillon, her father astonished and delighted her by revealing the same misgivings. "The people have a right to the land," he said. He planned to leave the army and stand somewhere as a Home Rule candidate. He had even drafted an election address.

Typhoid fever was endemic in Dublin of the '80's, and death took him from her before his resignation was made. For the second time she was orphaned, and now she was as if widowed also. She never ceased to mourn the still-young father whom strangers had often mistaken for her husband. In a sense, she was to search for him her whole life through.

3

If Thomas Gonne had lived, his daughter might have become a constitutional reformer like himself. As it was, banished to London and the mercies of Uncle William, head of the wine business, inevitably she became a revolutionary; for Uncle William was narrow and bigoted where Thomas had been liberal and humane. England, already seen as the oppressor of Ireland, became also the place of hated exile. She was confirmed in a lifelong detestation of England, whereas Ireland and France were both home.

London too had its troubles, there were demonstrations and marches of the unemployed. Escaping from Uncle William's gloomy house to watch a meeting in Trafalgar Square, she found herself invited up on to the platform by Tom Mann, and listened enthralled while he told his working-class audience that they were strong, if they would only realise their strength. Then a body of police advanced with drawn batons, and the crowd melted away. She was astonished and contemptuous, and it seemed to her that she had learnt two important facts: that the English were too poor-spirited and law-abiding to meet force with force, and that no revolution that shrank from force could hope to prevail.

As a disciplinary measure, Uncle William informed his nieces that their father had left them penniless and entirely

dependent upon himself. Maud defied him, applied to a
theatrical agency, and was engaged as leading lady for a
touring company, merely on the strength of a few Dublin
elocution lessons and her amazing looks. But she collapsed
with a haemorrhage while the plays were in rehearsal. Aunt
Mary from the Cook side, an altogether more sympathetic
relative, took charge of the sickbed and assured her that
William's story was a fabrication; she and Kathleen would
both have adequate private incomes when they came of age.
And undeniably it is easier to be a rebel when one has
comfortable means; but at least Maud had the satisfaction of
knowing that she had asserted her independence when
believing herself a pauper.

The wicked uncle's spell was broken. The threat of tuberculosis, from which her mother had died, meant release for
Maud, and Aunt Mary took her to Royat in the Auvergne,
where the doctor had advised a cure. The weather there was
oppressive, breaking at last in a great thunderstorm; and at
its height, symbolically enough, she met the great love of her
life.

He was Lucien Millevoye, politician and journalist, and a
poet's grandson; he was ill like herself, and melancholy from
the breakdown of his marriage. In every respect he was
her complement; tall, dark, older (he was in his mid-thirties),
a passionate patriot whose whole ambition was to see France
win back Alsace-Lorraine, a bonny hater of the English
("Germany is only the incidental, England is the hereditary
enemy of France"). A photograph of this time shows him as
a fine-looking man, with visionary dark eyes and short pointed
beard; he bears a certain resemblance to Parnell.

Every day at the springs they met and talked, and he told
her of the hopes he was pinning on General Boulanger, who
was to be the new architect of French greatness, the new
Napoleon. In return she confided the failure of her plan to
go on the stage, and found that he considered it an ambition
quite unworthy of her. He was convinced that if she only

understood her own power, she could free Ireland as Joan of
Arc freed France. He proposed an alliance: they would work
together for Irish freedom and the regaining of Alsace-
Lorraine. She accepted in a glow of fervour. Here was her
direction in life; here was a friendship which would not
diminish her into domestic mediocrity, but increase her
strength in the cause of liberty.

Finally free from Aunt Mary's nominal tutelage, she was
presented to the General; but even to her inexperienced eye
he looked more like an operatic tenor than a Napoleon, and
he appeared more absorbed by his mistress, Mme de
Bonnemains, than by the future of Alsace-Lorraine. However, his party were becoming powerful, and they had
proposals for a treaty with Russia which they wanted taken
secretly to St. Petersburg. Millevoye asked her to act as
messenger, and off she went, documents in dress and
revolver in pocket. It was the kind of sensational assignment
that appealed to what one is tempted to call her silly side.
But this tendency to dramatise life, which she herself freely
admitted, was also what gave her her incomparable dash and
verve when there was a genuinely important task in hand.

The important task now was to return to Ireland and find
some place in the nationalist struggle, and here she came up
against the blank wall of Irish anti-feminism. Davitt,
cornered at the House of Commons, was cold and discouraging, taking her for a spy. Dublin gave her a warmer
personal welcome, but her friends at first were chiefly those
she had known through her father. None of the nationalist
organisations would admit women.

There had been a Ladies' Land League under Anna Parnell, the leader's sister, which had done gallant work while he
and his lieutenants were in gaol, agitating not only on their
behalf but for the "Treason Felony" prisoners who had tried
to blow up the House of Commons and London Bridge.
Members had collected funds for a weekly grant to the
prisoners' families, had provided legal defence for those

arrested, had built huts for those evicted. Their reward was
to be disbanded by Parnell as soon as he came out of Kilmainham Gaol. Against the popular idealisation of Parnell
as a great lover must be set this shabby treatment of his
gifted sister and her fellow-patriots. They were not so
necessary to his comfort as was Mrs. O'Shea.

But if there was no official body to which Maud Gonne
could belong, at least she soon knew a circle of like-minded
people, chief among them the old Fenian leader John
O'Leary, now a gentle elder-statesman of both the Nationalist and the Celtic-revival movements. It was O'Leary who
made known to her the work of the young poet Willie Yeats,
and though not really very capable of literary appreciation,
she wept over passages in *The Wanderings of Oisin* and perceived that here was a talent that could usefully be harnessed
to the cause. O'Leary gave her a letter of introduction to the
Yeats family, then living in London, and she called on them
in January of 1889, on her way back to Paris to report progress to her Boulangist ally.

She astounded the family by her looks, her outspokenness
and her French elegance, and made a conquest of Willie as
immediate as it was to prove permanent; but so little did the
event impress itself on her memory that she afterwards
believed she had met him for the first time at the O'Learys'
in Dublin. His letters to O'Leary and to Katharine Tynan,
however, make it clear that this was the first time he had seen
her. Yeats is a figure of such towering importance, and Maud
Gonne was for so long the centre of his life, that none of his
numerous biographers seem to have realised how far away
he was from the centre of hers.

She liked him, however. She found in him, as Katharine
Tynan had already done, an engaging combination of
intellectual self-confidence and emotional diffidence. She
was charmed by the ease with which she could fire his
enthusiasm, flattered when he proposed to write a poetic play
on the liberation of Ireland in which she should take the

chief part. He was barely older than herself, and beside a man of the world like Millevoye must have seemed a mere boy. It would not occur to her to consider him a serious suitor, or to warn him that he was besieging a pre-engaged heart.

4

Without authority or position, she was nevertheless soon known in Dublin, the superb young woman in the Paris clothes, uniquely free to please herself, and riding alone on an outside car—unheard-of thing—with no more escort than a huge Great Dane. She and Dagda were inseparable. Sometimes his presence was objected to, in trains or restaurants, or on the platform at meetings. "Remove him then," would say Miss Gonne with a smile, but nobody braved the great beast.

She took a furnished flat above a bookshop in Nassau Street, and it became a centre for O'Leary's group of young writers and revolutionaries. Arthur Griffith was an early friend, a quiet, shy boy, giving little hint that he would one day be at the helm. Presently Dublin Castle honoured her with the attentions of a C.I.D. sleuth, and much entertainment could be had in giving this individual the slip, in the shops of Grafton Street, or by melting into the poor back streets where she was sure of protectors.

Tim Harrington, one of the Parnellite M.P.s, persuaded her that she could speak in public, and she found it was true. She had the gift to hold a crowd, and her stage training enabled her to project her voice effortlessly, even in the open air. (Miss Horniman's "beautiful woman shrieking from a cart" is a piece of petulance; there is plenty of evidence that

she did not need to shriek.) It was Harrington who arranged
for her to visit Donegal, where a particularly brutal eviction
campaign was in progress. Her last scruples about the use of
force vanished as she saw old people or mothers with babies
put out to lie under hedges, or herded into workhouses. "A
thousand Irish men, women and children were left home-
less," she writes, "and how many of them died that winter I
do not know. I have always hated war and am by nature and
philosophy a pacifist, but it is the English who forced war on
us, and the first principle of war is to kill the enemy."

There was no force as yet available, but she did what she
could, helping to build huts for the evicted, distributing her
own money and the largesse of importunate admirers, turning on her Daughter of the Garrison manner to bluff the
police into releasing demonstrators. She found allies in many
of the parish priests, and began to see their faith as something
that she could share. The scandal of the evictions had roused
English indignation also, but her English sympathisers looked
for a cure to a change of heart at Westminster. She, on the
contrary, was more and more convinced that English govern-
ments of whatever complexion would always side with the
landlords, and that only in an independent, republican
Ireland could the peasant know security.

Her other major concern was the fate of the twenty-seven
Treason Felony prisoners in Portland Gaol. News had leaked
out of the terrible conditions which had already driven five
of them insane. Distance and poverty made it impossible for
their families to visit them, and although Amnesty Associations had been formed in Dublin, Galway and London, the
fact that Parnell had disowned them made it almost impossible to get publicity on their behalf.

She applied to the Home Secretary for permits to visit
eight of the prisoners as representative of their families, and
once again her bluff succeeded. What she saw left an in-
delible mark of horror on her mind; the plight of prisoners,
all prisoners, was to haunt her for the rest of her life. Some

power seemed to speak through her, and she promised these wrecks of men release, naming the order, and the length of time each one still had to serve. In every case her prophecy came true.

The episode as recounted in her autobiography is intensely moving; it also gives, I am sure unwittingly, the impression that she secured their release single-handed. This of course was not so; many men and women of goodwill shared in the effort. Her role was to put fresh heart into them, as she had into the priests and the Land Leaguers fighting eviction, and as she would presently do for the rebuffed and discarded women of the liberation movement.

She was not an originator, not a thinker or a planner or in the long run even a leader, but she was an inspiration, a flame. She brought to what looked like hopeless causes a courage and generosity which were her own, and wealth and position which, she was the first to acknowledge, were the result of sheer good luck. But other young women blessed with similar luck never thought of sharing it beyond their immediate circle. At almost every turn in her life, Maud Gonne could have had an easy and cherished existence. It is infinitely to her credit that at every turn she deliberately chose to make it hard.

5

"The Woman of the Sidhe", they had begun to call her in Donegal, finding in her an all-powerful protectress whom even the English soldiers dared not oppose; and certainly she must have seemed to her adorers elusive as a fairy, flitting ceaselessly between Donegal, Dublin, London and Paris, and accompanied (in those happy pre-quarantine days) by innumerable birds in cages and by Dagda the Great Dane.

In London, Yeats was her principal friend, and when she could spare him a moment from her speaking and lobbying on behalf of the men in Portland, he endeavoured, at first successfully, to draw her into the occultism which was his chief interest after herself. She had always liked to fancy herself possessed of mystical powers, and frequently had premonitions and visions, in which a strong element of wishful thinking can be detected.

The "Order of the Golden Dawn" gave her silly side full scope, and she passed several initiations, but presently grew tired of it, observing that MacGregor Mathers and the other initiates were a moth-eaten lot. Willie's researches into Celtic mysticism, on the other hand, could be channelled into the cause of Irish freedom, and seemed altogether more promising to one who was now, as it were, an honorary member of the Sidhe.

She was back in Donegal for the eviction season of 1890, and this time she and her priest friends had a new technique to hold the people on the land and prevent them from drifting to the towns and the emigration ships. When a family had been evicted and its cabin battered down, some outlying farm was persuaded to shelter it, while she and her band of young men rebuilt the cabin. The police looked on helplessly; feeling against evictions was now running so high in England, as well as in Ireland, that authority dared not interfere. The reinstated families were welcomed home with torchlight processions, and each one increased the legend of her invincibility.

But if Yeats and the rest had accepted that she would flash in and out of their lives like a will-o'-the-wisp, Millevoye, the requited lover, was less patient. In his view, their "alliance" implied that she would stay in Paris and work for Ireland by remote control. He followed her to Donegal, falling ill at a wretched country inn, and she was obliged to break off her cabin-building and go to nurse him. "We quarrelled seriously," she admits. "He said things that, because of the truth there was in them, made me angry. I was killing myself and only fighting a side-issue. I would be doing more, stirring up indignation abroad and securing allies for Ireland." She was touched, and yet furious; no one should dictate to her, not even Millevoye. When he was fit to travel she packed him off home.

But it was a fact that she had started having haemorrhages again, and when word came that the English had a warrant out for her arrest, she listened to reason. A winter in gaol might be the end of her. Friends got her to the boat at Larne, with instructions not to stop anywhere till she was safely in France. There, her doctor was grave, and ordered a winter on the Riviera. St. Raphael was the place he recommended, then a tiny fishing village, where she could breathe the air of the sunny pinewoods all day, and burn a creosote lamp in her room at night. It appeared that Millevoye had been ordered to winter in St. Raphael also.

At what point the alliance of political friendship turned into an alliance between lovers one can, of course, only surmise, but it surely cannot have been later than this winter of peace and respite for them both. He had fully proved his devotion, and it was not his fault that he could not marry her; he was unable to secure a divorce from his wife. In their own eyes they must have been as if married. Nevertheless concealment was necessary, not on his part but on hers. She was a public figure in Puritan Ireland, and already the object of speculation and gossip, as a young woman with many admirers who seemed curiously unwilling to accept any of them. For the sake of Ireland and the cause she must keep her liaison secret; but to one with her natural frankness of character, putting herself in an equivocal position went sorely against the grain.

However, there was nothing in St. Raphael to spoil their idyll. No one knew who they were or cared what they did. They walked, rode, picnicked in the woods, and she regained her health fast. In the evenings, he wrote propaganda articles for the Boulangists and suggested she should do the same for Ireland. She sent a description of the evictions to a Paris review and it was accepted; she had the excitement of discovering in herself yet another capacity. She might not be a literary type like Willie, but she could write the sort of tough polemical article that would be published, and read. A rather more dangerous lesson learned from Millevoye was that propaganda for a cause in which one passionately believed was not necessarily compatible with a strict regard for fact.

Opening a letter from Willie one day, she found the exquisite poem beginning "I dreamt that one had died in a strange place . . ." She was greatly amused, though one may hope that she was slightly remorseful also. Far from dying, she was living in every sense—as patriot, propagandist, woman—more fully than ever before.

The significance of the Parnell divorce seems to have passed her by. The thoughts of both of them were on Boulanger, whose star was in the ascendant; they could hope that he would soon hold France in his hand. In the spring came his principal lieutenant, Paul Déroulède, who had been organising a "Ligue des Patriotes" in the south of France, and was perhaps anxious to know what kept Millevoye so long from the centre of affairs. For once, she made no conquest; they did not like each other. He shared Millevoye's determination to regain Alsace-Lorraine, but he thought that an alliance with England against Germany was France's surest means to this end. She suddenly found herself quite cured, returned to Paris and took a little flat. Much as she loved Millevoye, work for Ireland came first, and if he would not help her she must carry it forward alone.

She flirted with the Irish Jacobite families living in Paris, but found them altogether too aloof, aristocratic, and prone to dwell in the past. Her appeal, as always, was to the young. She was soon in demand as lecturer to student groups—

Catholic, Republican, it made no difference—and fired them with her stories of English inhumanity, the evicted families sleeping in the heather, the Irish political prisoners rotting for years in the cold hell of Queen Victoria's gaols.

In the summer of 1891 she was back in Dublin. Yeats came over on holiday, and could sense some personal disappointment behind her febrile activity. It would have been honest to tell him the truth, but it would also have been unwise. He was, as his friend and biographer J. M. Hone has admitted, notoriously unable to keep a secret. She had to let him fancy her trouble was something he could cure, and to refuse a proposal of marriage as kindly as she knew how.

But it was always her gift to keep the friendship of a disappointed suitor. They walked the cliff-paths of Howth, and he read her his poetic play *The Countess Cathleen*, in which figured strong elements of her Donegal legend. He begged her, if he could find a producer, to take the part of the Countess, which had of course been written with her in mind. She was sorely tempted, and for that reason refused. The theatre, if she were to return to it, might well become a passion, and no more than love could it be allowed to deflect her from her real work.

News from France recalled her in a hurry. The operatic General Boulanger had proved to be no more than a hero of soap-opera. Having muffed every political chance, he had found himself unable to endure existence after the untimely death of Mme de Bonnemains, and had committed a histrionic suicide on her grave.

And next month, death laid its hand on the great Irish leader also. By a strange coincidence, Maud Gonne was on the boat which bore his corpse back to Ireland. She was linked in friendship with Davitt, Harrington and other Parnellite M.P.s, but she had little feeling for Parnell himself. He had alienated her by his repudiation of physical force, and of the Treason Felony prisoners, and by his treatment of the Ladies' Land League. Like thousands of others

B

she was moved as she stood in the cemetery of Glasnevin and saw the falling star, but her chief thought was: "the Parliamentary Party was dead before Parnell and should have been buried with him." For his successor, the unfortunate Redmond, she was to feel nothing but contempt.

What she could hardly guess at was the profoundly traumatic effect which the loss of Parnell was to have on the liberation movement, deflecting the interest of the young intellectuals away from politics and towards literature and the arts. It made an immediate difference to the aims and attitudes of many among her friends; but it made none at all to hers.

6

Once Millevoye had inspired her; now it was her turn to reanimate him. He was so utterly discouraged after the death of Boulanger that he planned to leave political life, saying he was too old to make a fresh start. But she knew that his gifts as a journalist could still serve the "alliance", even though his chance of political office had gone. It was she who made him take up the editorship of *La Patrie*, an evening paper owned by the director of one of the big Paris shops. "I had put my whole will," she says, "into making him regain confidence in himself, and realise that, with his wonderful power of literary expression, he would be able to make that little-read paper into an instrument with which to rebuild the shattered fortunes of his party and regain his old influence." For the time being, at any rate, she also regained hers with Millevoye, and most of the articles in which *La Patrie* denounced "les atrocités dans les bagnes anglais", though signed by the editor, were in fact written by her.

But he was not her only mouthpiece. She also developed what she calls "a sort of press agency for Ireland in Paris" and in time this became a little sub-editor's sheet, *L'Irlande Libre*, which was circulated to all the French newspapers, and from which they could take material without charge. What with this, and the reports of her lectures, she calculated that she got some two thousand items a year into the French press.

"This period of my life was one of ceaseless activity and travelling," she records. "I rarely spent a month in the same place." Spurring on the Amnesty Associations in England and Scotland; house-building for the evicted in Ireland; lecturing in France and Holland; then in the winter of 1894-5 making a lecture tour of America and collecting over a thousand pounds for the prisoners' dependents—besides reading the Clan na Gael an extra lecture on the necessity of healing its own rifts and getting on with the job of fighting the British Empire—it seems incredible that any one person, before the days of air travel, could have accomplished so much.

The seal of recognition was set on her activities when Asquith sent for Redmond and told him they must stop. Redmond answered truthfully that neither he nor anyone else had the slightest authority over Miss Gonne; she acted entirely on her own initiative, and he felt sure the only way to silence her was to set the Portland prisoners free. And shortly after her return from America they were, in fact, released.

There are two episodes of these crowded years which she does not relate. Between 1893 and 1895 she bore Millevoye two children. The first died in infancy; the second, a daughter, was named Iseult.

She was a devoted mother, and kept the child with her, presenting her variously as "my adopted daughter" and "my niece", and later on, more grandly, as "my kinswoman". Iseult also, perforce, adopted this last mediaeval-sounding phrase, while deeply resenting the fact that she was never openly acknowledged by the mother she adored.

Few in Ireland were deceived by any of this elaborate pretence; in any case, as the child grew up, her resemblance to her lovely mother was too striking to be missed. Nor did many seriously doubt that Millevoye was the father. But she had given a handle to her enemies, and the legend that Maud Gonne "was free with her favours" and "led a fast life in Paris" is current to this day. An honourable and indeed tragic relationship between two dedicated idealists was debased by a secrecy which was no doubt inevitable in its day and age, but which must surely always fail of its effect.

7

When she visited Ireland now, she found literary and dramatic ideas almost jostling political ones off the stage. In long walks over the Dublin hillsides, Willie outlined his plan of a great literary movement for the glory of Ireland. He told her, she recalls, that "if only we could make contact with the hidden forces of the land it would give us strength for the freeing of Ireland. Most of our talk centred round this and it led us both into strange places, from which I, less daring in thought if more daring in action than Willie, drew back, lest it might lead me away and not into the heart of Ireland's hidden strength." Peering into the Celtic twilight was only allowable if it gave one the incentive to plan a less misty future. The ancient heroic epics must be used to put fresh heart into one's contemporaries. The moment the bogey of art-for-art's-sake raised its head, she would have none of it.

In *Scattering Branches*, a collection of tributes written after Yeats's death, she looks back on their work together in these

years. "He hated crowds, I loved them. His generous desire
to help and share my work brought him into contact with
crowds and with all sorts of people, men from the country
and men from the towns, working for Ireland's freedom. I
hardly realised then how important that contact was for
him, and sometimes felt guilty at taking so much of his time
from his literary work. . . . I remember Willie's astonished
pleasure when, after a meeting, some shy boy would come up
and shake his hand because he had read his poems and loved
them; I knew that contact was good for him. After my
marriage and during my long sojourn in France, he lost this
contact and became more unaware of the forces working for
Ireland's freedom."

There was nothing dog-in-the-manger in her attitude to
him or any other admirer. She was glad that he should make
new friends, who could give him a more literary sympathy:
Mrs. Shakespear, the London solicitor's wife who was his
regular correspondent, and Lady Gregory, offering him the
peace, beauty and relative luxury of summers at Coole.

She and Lady Gregory did not take to each other, and if it
is true that Lady Gregory asked her "intentions" in regard to
Yeats (a story, it must be remembered, which rests entirely
on Maud Gonne's evidence) then she certainly deserved the
crushing snub with which the story concludes.

But there is no reason to doubt Maud Gonne's sincerity
when she says that at this time she welcomed the friendship,
and felt nothing but goodwill towards the plans for a revival
of Irish drama presently hatching at Coole. She saw them
as a part of the nationalist struggle, as indeed for a time
they were. And when in the early years of the new century
Lady Gregory published her two books of epic translation,
Maud Gonne was among their keenest readers, admitting
that they were "a real joy to people like myself who were
unable to read the old Irish texts".

But her heart was with the true revolutionaries, particularly Arthur Griffith, the radical journalist, and James

Connolly, the tough young labour leader. Griffith had founded his fierce little weekly the *United Irishman* with a capital of £30, and owing to its frequent seizures by the Government it was for ever in financial trouble. Connolly was even further to the left than herself, in fact a Marxist, and at first she was a trifle wary of him. But she never could resist revolutionary fervour, and soon he was enshrined in her estimation as "the bravest man I know".

Connolly and Griffith were moving spirits in the 1898 Centenary Committee, formed to commemorate the Rising of 1798 and to put the Separatist idea anew before the people. Early in 1897 she was sent to Mayo on Centenary work, and at the same time asked by Connolly to investigate near-famine conditions over which the British Government was busily throwing a veil. The potato had failed again, and the people must be roused to save themselves, and not die as in 1847. Together they drafted a leaflet claiming that starving people had the right to take food wherever they might find it. It was the prelude to what was perhaps the most dramatic campaign of her agitator's career.

She arrived in Mayo to find conditions ominously like 1847; the people listless and apathetic from hunger, famine fever spreading, doctors signing certificates of death from "heart failure". Relief work consisted of a little desultory road making, for which only one member of each family was eligible, and for which he was paid sixpence a day.

She sat down immediately and wrote articles for two Dublin papers, appealing for subscriptions, and these provided a little food for immediate relief. She bought oatmeal and condensed milk out of her own pocket, and set the women to cooking and distributing porridge. She urged the men to take the law into their own hands and steal sheep off the hills, but the native honesty was too deeply ingrained and few would stir. But they accepted her leaflets, and agreed to attend a mass meeting in the centre of Belmullet, though for those on relief work it meant losing even the miserable daily sixpence. As before in Donegal, she found allies in the priests, and the parish priest of Belmullet agreed to take the chair.

He helped her to draw up a list of minimum demands: the sixpence a day to be raised to a shilling, an immediate free distribution of seed potatoes, relief payments extended to cover the planting of them. Next day, ten thousand people from the whole countryside crowded into Belmullet, the biggest gathering the town had ever seen, a quiet, anxious crowd of ragged men and women, with twenty constables looking on. She told them that they were cowards if they allowed their children to die, that she was about to present their demands to the Board of Guardians in session in the Court House, and that they must be ready to back her up.

She confronted the Board, which included two officials from Dublin Castle, and found them truculent; her demands were absurd. She replied that the people were desperate and dying, and that if they died, she would see to it that they died fighting. Ten thousand people could soon take the guns from twenty policemen, and it would be two or three days before reinforcements could arrive. Outside, she could hear the murmur of the crowd, and the strange soft sound of bare feet beating on the hard earth.

It was an anxious moment, for she had already seen that starving people are not the best material for a fight. Would the Guardians call her bluff? But she had scared them. They conferred together, then agreed to her demands; relief should be raised to six shillings a week, and seed potatoes fetched from Scotland. Apparently no one had thought, any more than in 1847, of taking this obvious step.

Victory was announced to a crowd hysterical with astonishment and gratitude, and she rubbed the lesson home—they had done it themselves, by defying the overseers and turning up in such numbers, and what resolution and defiance had done once could be repeated. "You have won these small things by your numbers and by your united strength.

By your strength and courage you must win the freedom of Ireland."

She went back to Dublin and secured the promise of a fish-curing plant for the worst-hit of the fishing villages, then spent the next two months in Mayo, organising nursing and school meals. This time, there had been no organisation behind her. She had stopped a famine single-handed. It is permissible to wonder what effect she could have had if she had been at the height of her powers in '47. Might not her name be as widely renowned as Florence Nightingale's?

8

It was Jubilee summer, and the Nationalists were determined that Dublin at any rate should not appear wholeheartedly loyal to the ageing Queen. Corporation workmen cut the wires and prevented the illumination of Unionist shops. Connolly made a big coffin to symbolise the fate of the British Empire, and Maud Gonne set her women friends to the sewing of flags inscribed with the crimes of the reign—the numbers dead of famine, the numbers of houses destroyed, the numbers of men in gaol.

The convention of the Centenary Committees was arranged for the afternoon of Jubilee Day, and she sat at the executive table beside Yeats, anxiously listening for the sounds of Connolly's procession. When its band was heard, they rushed out, and found it headed by a rickety handcart in the shape of a hearse bearing the coffin, and escorted by a delighted crowd. They joined in, and the procession arrived on O'Connell Bridge where the coffin was ceremonially flung into the Liffey. Police baton charges followed, people were hurt and one old woman killed. Connolly and several others were arrested, but next morning she got Harrington to defend them, and all were released. The Dublin anti-Jubilee riots made headlines all over the world, and she was triumphant. English Socialists had told her that they, too, planned demonstrations, but she heard of none, and once more she was confirmed in her opinion: the English working-classes had no real fight in them.

Yeats had stood by her bravely, but he was inwardly shocked by all this mob violence. He could not share her feeling that they were now in truth "tapping Ireland's hidden strength". Together they made a tour of the Irish communities in Scotland, speaking on behalf of the Centenary Association, and he described it as the worst ordeal of his life, though the experience of facing hecklers was to stand him in good stead when he came to direct a theatre.

He tried to lead her thoughts into the gentler path of mysticism. In January of 1898 he reported to George Russell that "Maud Gonne and myself are going for a week or two perhaps to some country place in Ireland, to get as you do the forms of gods and spirits and to get sacred earth for our evocation. Perhaps we can arrange to go somewhere where you are, so that we can all work together. Maud Gonne has seen a vision of a little temple of the heroes which she proposes to build somewhere in Ireland when '98 is over and to make the centre of our mystical and literary movement." This, he felt sure, was the real Maud Gonne, and not the terrible lioness inciting crowds to smash windows. He was mistaken; it was the Temple of the Heroes, and not Connolly's coffin, which represented her silly side.

After all this excitement, the actual '98 celebrations came as an anti-climax. In order to present a united front, Redmond and the Parliamentarians were invited to join the platform party; this disgusted Maud Gonne, and she refused to appear. The true value of the Centenary work, in her view, had been to do propaganda for separatism in country districts, and to awaken long dormant national pride. A large part of the spade-work had fallen to the women supporters, and more than ever she resented the fact that there were no political organisations open to them. She resolved that presently she would form one of her own.

When she first came to Dublin her following was mostly male, but by now she had a devoted band of women friends. Not the least remarkable facet of her charm was that it operated equally well on either sex. Katharine Tynan comments: "I remember when the heads of all my male friends, young and old, were flustered by her beauty and grace. But they soon got over it. I have always held that love must have something to live upon, something of invitation if not of response. Her aloofness must have chilled the most ardent lover." One may also perhaps surmise that for the general run of 19th-century Irishmen, undernourished and under-sized, it would not have been convenient to love a goddess six feet high.

There is a charming picture in Maud Gonne's memoirs of summer sailing trips to Ireland's Eye, with her friends Helena Molony, Maureen Fox, Susan Varian and Ella Young. They revived on the island the ancient rites of Celtic mythology, and lit Beltaine fires. In Paris, she could draw on similar loyalty from gifted women writers like Louise Stratenius and Ghenia de Sainte-Croix, who did their gallant best to carry on *L'Irlande Libre* during her lengthy absences in Ireland.

It was they who warned her that she should look to her French defences, that she was too much from home. The pro-English party, headed by the formidable Clemenceau, wanted to end her thirteen years' association with Millevoye, and swing the powerful voice of *La Patrie* round to their viewpoint. They had even selected an instrument for the purpose, an opera singer whose talents Millevoye considered insufficiently appreciated.

Yeats, visiting Maud Gonne in Paris in February of 1899, found her unwontedly spiritless and sad. As few of the letters which passed between them seem to have survived, it is not possible to say whether he already knew the full truth about the parentage of Iseult, but his letter to Lady Gregory suggests that all was now confided. ". . . she has told the story of her life, telling gradually, in more detail, all except a few things which I can see are too painful for her to talk of and about which I do not ask her. I do not wonder that she shrinks from life. Hers has been in part the war of phantasy and of a blinded idealism against eternal law."

Later that spring the blow fell. An article appeared in *La Patrie* which seemed to her the negation of all they had worked for, an appeal for the return of Alsace-Lorraine which named Germany as the one and only enemy and made no mention of England. Taxed, Millevoye admitted that though he had signed it, the opera singer had written it; in his turn he upbraided her for her absurd devotion to the Irish revolutionaries. She faced the fact that for all his French patriotism, he had never cared a fig for Irish liberation; it had merely been a bait to keep her with him. Ireland to him was the gloomy little country where he had nearly died of pneumonia. Whether or no he had betrayed her with the opera singer, he had betrayed what she valued far more, the darling object of her life. The alliance was at an end.

It was like her to break it off cleanly, ruthlessly, without possibility of repair. Moving as they did in the same political circles, they were bound to meet again, but they met as enemies. She cut him out of her life, and she suffered deeply. It is doubtful if she ever quite cut him out of her heart.

When Yeats found her, weary and travel-stained, at her sister's London flat, he again begged her to let him take care of her; but although she was soon to commit a great matrimonial folly, it was not the folly of marrying him. She was well aware that though he talked of cherishing and protecting it is the privilege of genius to be cherished and protected, and that if he were ever to take a wife, she must be a woman who would sink her interests utterly in his.

"You make beautiful poetry out of what you call your un-happiness," she told him, "and you are happy in that. Marriage would be such a dull affair. Poets should never marry. The world should thank me for not marrying you."

9

The course of history left her no time for repining. The Boer War gave the Nationalists the chance to put into practice their oft-repeated slogan that "England's difficulty is Ireland's opportunity". Redmond and the Parliamentarians were pro-British, the Nationalists violently pro-Boer. Preventing enlistment in the British Army, encouraging enlistment in the Irish Brigade presently formed under Colonel Blake to fight on the Boer side—these were activities for which Griffith and the *United Irishman* started an intense campaign, and in which nationalistic Irishwomen, debarred and disregarded ever since the Ladies' Land League, could play an effective part.

Maud Gonne hurried on her plans for a revolutionary women's society. The Celtic Literary Society lent her their rooms at 32 Lower Abbey Street, and there on Easter Sunday of 1900 a small but warlike group brought it into being, with herself as president, Maire Quinn as secretary, and the sisters of Griffith and Willie Rooney on the committee. They christened themselves Inghinidhe na hEireann, the Daughters of Erin.

Inghinidhe went into action at once, with leaflets urging Irishwomen not to consort with soldiers of their country's enemy. These were distributed to girls walking arm-in-arm with Tommies in the Dublin streets. It took courage, and brothers or sweethearts had to come out in defence;

O'Connell Street was the scene of many battles. But excitement served to kindle enthusiasm, and the numbers of the Daughters increased.

To inspire recruiting, a Dublin visit by the ageing Victoria was arranged for that spring, and denounced by the Nationalists. *L'Irlande Libre* carried a front-page cartoon of the Queen in a shamrock gown, gazing on the dead who rose from their graves and pointed accusing fingers at her, the roofless walls of what had been their houses behind them. The principal article, "Reine de la Disette", was written by Maud, and Griffith caused her to translate it and published it, as "The Famine Queen", in the *United Irishman* for April 7th. It merits quotation at some length, as the most famous of her political articles and the most characteristic of her polemical style:

And in truth for Victoria, in the decrepitude of her 81 years, to have decided after an absence of half a century to revisit the country she hates and whose inhabitants are the victims of the criminal policy of her reign, the survivors of 60 years of organised famine, the political necessity must have been terribly strong; for after all she is a woman, and however vile and selfish and pitiless her soul may be, she must sometimes tremble as death approaches when she thinks of the countless Irish mothers who, shelterless under the cloudy Irish sky, watching their starving little ones, have cursed her before they died.

Every eviction during 63 years has been carried out in Victoria's name, and if there is a Justice in Heaven the shame of these poor Irish emigrant girls, whose very innocence makes them an easy prey and who have been overcome in the terrible struggle for existence on a foreign shore, will fall on this woman, whose bourgeoise virtue is so boasted, and in whose name their homes were destroyed. . . .

England is in decadence. The men who formerly made her greatness, the men from the country districts, have disappeared, they have been swallowed up by the great black manufacturing cities; they have been flung into the crucible where gold is made. Today the giants of England are the giants of finance and of the Stock Exchange, who have risen to power on the backs of a struggling mass of pale, exhausted slaves.

The storm approaches, the gold which the English have made out of the blood and tears of millions of human beings attracts the covetousness of the world. Who will aid the pirates to keep their spoil? In their terror they turn to Victoria, their Queen. She has succeeded in amassing more gold than any of her subjects, she has always been ready to cover with her royal mantle the crimes and turpitude of her Empire, and now, trembling on the brink of the grave, she rises once more at their call. . . . Taking the Shamrock in her withered hand, she dares to ask Ireland for soldiers —for soldiers to fight for the exterminators of their race!

And the reply of Ireland comes sadly but proudly, not through the lips of the miserable little politicians who are touched by the English canker, but through the lips of the Irish people:

Queen, return to your own land; you will find no more Irishmen ready to wear the red shame of your livery. In the past they have done so from ignorance, and because it is hard to die of hunger when one is young and strong and the sun shines, but they shall do so no longer. See! your recruiting agents return alone and unsuccessful from my green hills and plains, because once more hope has revived, and it will be in the ranks of your enemies that my children will find employment and honour.

In the following weeks she returned to the attack, supported by Yeats; a brave gesture on his part, since it caused the withdrawal of a good many subscriptions to his Literary Theatre. His denunciation of the Queen was on rather different grounds from hers; he found that little was known of Victoria save that "she has certainly used her example and influence to cherish mediocrity in music and in painting and in literature".

The royal visit took place, and its highlight was a treat

to 15,000 schoolchildren in Phoenix Park. The Nationalists could scarcely interfere with the children's pleasure, but Inghinidhe announced that a Patriotic Treat would be given in July to all children who had not attended the Queen's. A subscription list was opened, and the Society spent two months of frenzied preparation, aided by young men from the Athletic Clubs named after the new hero, Major John MacBride.

Finally, on the first Sunday in July, Maud Gonne and Maire Quinn on an outside car led a two-mile-long procession of children to Clonturk Park, where there were games, racing, and hurling, and every child got a bag of cakes and sweets. Miss Gonne addressed the children towards the end of the afternoon, asking the boys never to disgrace themselves by joining the English army, navy or police, and the girls to use the influence they would have with brothers, sweethearts and husbands to further the National ideal.

"Dublin has never witnessed anything so marvellous as the procession of the 30,000 schoolchildren who refused to be bribed into parading before the Queen of England," the *United Irishman* declared. Its report might be biassed, but the Patriotic Treat certainly made an impression far deeper than the event itself seemed to warrant. It was the biggest thing yet organised by the Nationalists, and it proved to them that they *could* organise; many saw in the children's beanfeast of today the armed insurrection of a few years hence.

Maud Gonne was showered with grateful letters; a bricklayer wrote that "her services to the land of the Shamrock have been unparalleled, and there is no name that will ever shine out with greater prominence in the history of our country than that of our beloved lady, Miss Maud Gonne". To crown her triumph, the *Daily Express* in England was screaming for her arrest. And even when she was an old woman, people would come up to her and say: "I was a Patriotic Child at your party, the year the old Queen was over."

10

She had joined the Irish Republican Brotherhood, a secret society dating back to Fenian days, partly, she says, for a joke; but cloak-and-dagger intrigue always brought out the worst in her, as was shown by the plan she now laid before her fellow members. Inghinidhe had dealt a serious blow to recruitment; if one or two transport ships on their way to South Africa went to the bottom it might dry up altogether. Her French friends would manufacture bombs disguised as lumps of coal, and the I.R.B. would get them into the holds of ships. This fantastic idea was accepted, not only by the I.R.B., but what was more remarkable, by the Transvaal representative in Europe, who advanced £2,000 to cover the cost of making the bombs and getting the agents away to America afterwards.

The information, and the £2,000, were intercepted by the British secret service, and Maud Gonne faced the ruin of all her plans for a Franco-Irish alliance. She had also to face a painful interview with Millevoye, who rubbed in his "I told you so" with the venom of a lover discarded. As only the I.R.B. in Ireland had known of the plan, it seemed probable that one of them had betrayed her; she resigned her membership, and had no more dealings with secret societies. And for a time she banished herself from Paris, leaving Iseult at the flat in the care of a governess, and taking a little furnished house in the Dublin suburbs.

The episode had a steadying effect, and she went soberly to work under Griffith, acting as link between him and Connolly and the labour movement on the one hand, and between him and Yeats and the literary and dramatic societies on the other. The aim was to co-ordinate all the nationalist societies into an open separatist movement, and together she and Griffith drew up a programme which was ultimately to develop into Sinn Fein.

Inghinidhe, her own child, was growing fast; soon it had branches in Cork, Limerick and Ballina. Its programme was not so different from that of the Gaelic League; there were debates, Irish-language classes, free lessons in Irish history for children, amateur dramatics. But whereas the Gaelic League was, or was supposed to be, non-political, the ardent young woman who joined Inghinidhe could feel that everything she did there went to further the cause of an independent Ireland, and that week by week she was arming herself for the fight.

And all that the Daughters of Erin did was animated by the galvanic personality of their leader, lovely as ever, and therefore safe from the gibes about sour grapes incurred by other feminist agitators. Inghinidhe was bathed in her glamour—that much-abused word can be applied in sober truth to one who cast so potent a spell. Yeats wrote of her finely: "When men and women did her bidding they did it not only because she was beautiful, but because that beauty suggested joy and freedom." Into the rather humdrum middle-class lives of the girls who made up the society, she brought dedication and romance.

Its dramatic side was from the first strong, reflecting her own interest in the theatre, and it was to weave an important strand into the story of the Abbey. Plays on Irish subjects were put on when they could be found, which was seldom, but failing these, members mounted evenings of *tableaux vivants*, illustrating great moments of Irish history or patriotic songs, while somebody recited and the political lesson was driven home.

Maud Gonne knew the Fay brothers, Frank and Willie, because Frank contributed dramatic criticism to the *United Irishman*, and she begged them to coach her girls, as they were already coaching a mixed group of amateurs calling themselves the Ormonde Society. Yeats, coming in to watch rehearsals, was impressed by the Fays, their earnestness and knowledge of stage technique, and the results they were getting out of untried amateurs; and he realised that this was a better answer than the bringing over of professional companies from England, as had been done for three years running with no marked success.

The dramatic class of Inghinidhe provided the Abbey Theatre with its greatest leading lady, Sara Allgood, and also with its first, Maire nic Shiubhlaigh, who began life as Mary Walker and was the first player to turn her name into Irish for the stage. In her memoirs, she has described the excitement when it was learned that the Fays had secured a two-act Deirdre play from A. E. (George Russell), and a one-act patriotic play from Yeats. The Ormonde and Inghinidhe groups were merged to produce them at St. Teresa's Hall.

And an equal excitement was felt by Maud Gonne when Yeats showed her the script of the "dream" which Lady Gregory had helped him to get into words, "of a cottage where there was well-being and firelight and talk of a marriage, and into the midst of that cottage there came an old woman in a long cloak. She was Ireland herself, that Kathleen ni Houlihan for whom so many songs have been sung and for whose sake so many have gone to their death."

Willie had done what she had always known he had it in him to do—written a propaganda play of the first magnitude, one which would be a clarion call to Irish youth for ever. In her view, *Kathleen ni Houlihan* was simply "the most perfect play ever written in Ireland". And though at first she maintained her resolution never to act again, Yeats now had an irresistible bargaining counter; either she took the part or he withdrew the play.

Two letters which she wrote to him while he was staying at Coole have survived among Lady Gregory's papers:

Maud Gonne to W.B.Y. Postmark Paris, February 3, 1902.

My dear Willie,

Many thanks for your letter, I am delighted to hear that you have given *Kathleen ni Houlihan* to Fay. Did you write him that I would act the part of Kathleen? Have you got another copy that you could let me have, as I would like to learn the words here and then go over them with you in London. If you haven't got a copy I will write to Fay to get one ready for me. They must begin rehearsing it without me—as they are very slow and take a great time rehearsing a play, and I would not be in Dublin long enough to do all that with them. I have a lot of work here, a lecture on the 4th, on the 14th and on the 20th of February, and another one on the 4th March, besides a lot of other work. Easter I think will be the best time for the plays—but I will write to Fay as soon as I hear from you what you have arranged with him.

The Society of St. Patrice* is having such a handsome and rich and comic row that I thought it best not to go to the assemblée générale this year, as I didn't want to take sides.

Macgregor† wrote to me, he wanted to see me, but I didn't answer his letter—I really can't afford to have charlatans about, people don't understand it.

Martin‡ [*sic*] is ridiculous, it is too provoking giving up the literary theatre.

I can't write more as friends have just come in to see me.

In haste, always your friend, Maud Gonne.

A letter of which an undated fragment survives is probably of the same period:

All I want of you is not to build up an imaginary wall of effort between yourself and life—for the rest the gods will arrange—for you are one of those they have chosen to do

* The Irish Jacobite society in Paris.
† Macgregor Mathers, leader of the Golden Dawn occult society.
‡ Edward Martyn had withdrawn his support from the Literary Theatre on the grounds that Yeats's play *The Countess Cathleen* was heretical.

their work. As for the possible chance of danger which you speak of for me, I am under the great shield of Lugh.* The day I am no longer protected, if that day comes, my work for Ireland will be over. I should not need *and could not accept* protection from any one, though I fully realise and understand the generous and unselfish thoughts which were in your heart and I love you for them. I am glad you are in the country with Lady Gregory, I am sure it is good for you to be with her and you will do beautiful work, there is a peace and restfulness [there] you need. I am in my whirlwind, but in the midst of that whirlwind is dead quiet calm which is peace too.

Always your friend, Maud Gonne.

Even so small a sample of her correspondence with him is illuminating. It bears out that her attitude was just as she describes it in her memoirs, affectionate, admiring, comradely, detached. She is careful to raise no false hopes (and at this moment his hopes were probably higher than they had ever been). She will accept no "protection" that might be construed as the privilege of a fiancé. She is exactly what she signs herself, "always your friend". Occasionally in his letters to Lady Gregory, Yeats liked to hint at moments of relenting, or at any rate of regret. I am convinced that this was wishful thinking, and that no such moments ever occurred.

The plays were given for the three nights of April 2nd, 3rd and 4th, 1902, the leading lady alone being accorded the title of "Miss" on the programme, although all were equally unpaid. St. Teresa's Hall was a tiny place, seating only three hundred, with no dressing-rooms, and so little space backstage that the cast had to wait jammed against the wall and holding their breaths. All were supposed to be in position before the audience arrived, but Maud Gonne continued her lordly disregard of production discipline by arriving late and sweeping through the auditorium in her

* Lugh, the sun-god in Gaelic mythology.

ghostly robes, thus creating a sensation even before the curtain went up.

It was as nothing, however, to the sensation she created on the stage. Few now living remember that famous first night, but those who do speak of it in awestruck tones. When Maud Gonne flung off the trappings of the bent crone and drew herself up to her full magnificent height, "the young girl with the walk of a queen", she became for all present, as she had long been for Yeats, a myth made flesh.

How good was she really? Yeats reported to Lady Gregory that she played the part "magnificently and with weird power". The *All-Ireland Review* said: "She could scarcely be said to act the part, she lived it. When she entered the little firelit room there came with her a sense of tragedy and the passion of deathless endeavour." Her political opponents put a rather different emphasis on the statement that she did not act, but was just "the well-known Nationalist orator" using the stage as her platform.

But Maire nic Shiubhlaigh, who took the part over from her and was to hand on the tradition of it to many generations of Kathleens, called it a triumph of restrained, sensitive acting, modelled her own performance on it, and declared to the end of her life that she had never seen it surpassed.

The little hall was full on the first night, and crowds were turned away on the other two; the standing-room was packed too full for anyone to move in the intervals. But there was no persuading the leading lady to extend the run. She had a more important engagement—to agitate against evictions on a Roscommon estate.

After this triumph, the dramatic society was re-formed on surer footing, with herself and Yeats as two of the vice-presidents, and yet another step in the direction of the Abbey had been taken. But if *Kathleen ni Houlihan* represented the fine flower of Yeats's association with Maud Gonne, it was also the stick she was ever afterwards to beat him with. If he could do it once, why not again? Why be side-tracked

into poetic dramas with no political message? It was the
fault of those silly women, Lady Gregory and Miss Horniman, with their doctrine of art for art's sake. What had
begun as an amused indifference towards them turned into
active hatred, and it was easy to spread the story that they
were both in love with him, which was why one of them was
spending her fortune turning the old Mechanics' Institute
in Abbey Street into a theatre, while the other kept open
house for him and his literary friends at Coole.

The rift between the political and artistic factions rapidly
widened. When in October of the next year the society
produced Synge's *Shadow of the Glen*, Maud Gonne walked
out of the first performance in protest. The wild poetry and
pathos of Nora's struggle for personal happiness meant
nothing to her, who had given up her personal happiness for
a political ideal. All she saw was a play in which Irish
peasants were mocked for making loveless marriages, and
their young wives applauded for escaping with lovers if they
could. Was that the way to convince the outside world
that the Irish were a responsible people, and politically
mature?

Griffith denounced the play in the *United Irishman* and
next week allowed Yeats to publish his statement of faith,
that the society was not prepared to undertake any propaganda save that of good art. This was followed by a scathing
rejoinder from Maud Gonne:

A play which will please the men and women of Ireland
who have sold their country for ease and wealth, who
fraternise with their country's oppressors or have taken
service under them, a play that will please the host of
English functionaries and the English garrison, is a play
which can never claim to be national literature. . . . The
centre of the national life is still among the poor and the
workers, they alone have been true to Ireland, they alone are
worthy and they alone are capable of fostering a national
literature and a national dream.

I I

These first years of the century were splendid ones, if she could only have been content. She was more influential than at any previous time, and doing, particularly through Inghinidhe, genuinely constructive work. The legends of the Patriotic Treat and of her appearances as Kathleen had spread far beyond those who had actually witnessed them. A great poet had celebrated her in verse already famous. She had come to personify revolutionary Ireland, even among those whom the prospect filled with dismay.

She had, moreover, given her hitherto fiercely individualistic life a ballast and discipline by becoming a Roman Catholic. She had long felt drawn to the church of the people, while Protestantism was associated with her own class, the oppressors. And if the Catholic bishops were lukewarm or even hostile to the nationalist cause, she had found a very different attitude among the ordinary priests, who had shown themselves staunch allies in her battles against evictions and famine.

A priest sympathetic to the Boulangists, Canon Dissard, had been a close friend from her early days in France, and it was he who finally effected her conversion and became her confessor. She was not, perhaps, a very orthodox Catholic, but there is no sign that she ever regretted the step, and in 1910 she became a member of the Third (secular) Order of St. Francis, a saint to whose teachings she was most strongly attracted.

But she was a still young and beautiful woman, she was to all intents and purposes a widow, and she was lonely. She wished to remarry. This time, however, she would avoid the mistake of choosing a man who could put any other cause before that of Ireland: not France, nor art, nor even herself. The obvious candidate was John MacBride, the man who had been the second in command of the Irish Brigade in the Boer War.

He was the glamour-hero of the nationalist movement, even as she was the heroine. They met in Paris at the end of 1900, when the war moved into its guerrilla phase and had no further need of foreign recruits, and she gave him a hero's welcome. She told an audience at Limerick shortly afterwards: "I consider that John MacBride has done more for Ireland by organising the Irish Brigade in the Transvaal than any living man. It saved Ireland's honour at a time when there was great need."

But she did not rush into any rash engagement. He courted her for two years, and they had ample time to know each other. He was a tall, soldierly man a year younger than herself, with red hair and moustache, and face burnt brickred by the South African sun. He was also, like many of his men, an unemployed and rather pitiful exile in Paris, liable to arrest if he returned to Ireland; and she did what she could to keep open house for them all. MacBride and she shared what was to be her last lecture-tour in America, he speaking on the work of the Brigade, and she trying to convince the Irish-Americans of the Clan na Gael that it was no good looking to Parliamentarians like Redmond and Dillon for Ireland's liberation.

She does not seem to have been in love, or to have had any illusions about him, though doubtless there was a physical attraction, over and above the womanly pity she felt for an unemployed hero, flung on the scrap-heap almost overnight. She knew that he was really nothing but a fighting machine, that his upbringing had been narrow, that his views on women were the Irish peasant ones, and that he was only likely to settle down with a woman who knew her subordinate place.

She heard the ghostly voice of her father warning her

against the marriage, and the far from ghostly voices of her
friends and many of MacBride's. Griffith, who esteemed
them both, wrote in distress: "For your own sakes and for the
sake of Ireland to whom you both belong, don't get married."
Little Iseult, now boarding at a convent school, wept jealous
tears. News of the engagement was a knock-out blow to
Yeats, who had a lecture to deliver, and went through it
like an automaton, unable afterwards to remember a word he
had said.

Perhaps the opposition was too solid; perhaps it constituted one of those challenges she had never been able to
resist. She laughed and shrugged her shoulders, in that
reckless gesture her friends knew well, and went ahead.

They were married on February 21st, 1903, at the church of
St. Honoré d'Eylau in Paris, by Father Van Hecke, former
chaplain to the Transvaal Brigade, who had come specially
from Belgium for the occasion. The bride wore "a costume of
electric blue"; the best man carried the green flag of the Irish
Brigade, and the bridesmaid the blue flag presented to the
Brigade by Inghinidhe, who also sent over the wedding-
breakfast table decoration of shamrocks and violets from
Dublin. Father Van Hecke in his speech at the feast celebrated
this matching of two heroic souls. "The bride was one of
those women who rise scarce once in a century to sacrifice
themselves for their country; the bridegroom he had seen
enduring the hardships and dangers of the battlefield, with
all that courage and gaiety which has long been traditional
with the Irishman in whatever clime he has had to fight."

The honeymoon was spent in Normandy, and from Bayeux
she thanked Lady Gregory for a letter of good wishes—a
social duty which it must have given Lady Gregory great
satisfaction to perform:

Dear Lady Gregory,

Forgive me for not before this having written to thank
you for your most kind and thoughtful letter—I appreciated your kindness very much. I was married at the

English Consulate, as well as at my parish church, so I think it is quite legal.

We had heard that there was a possibility of the English trying to arrest Major MacBride at the consulate—but I do not think it would have been really possible, as even if the consulate is English territory, which is doubtful, they could not have imprisoned him there for long, and once outside he would have been free. No such attempt was made. The Consul was rather rude and began asking irrelevant questions, but when Major MacBride refused to answer, and told him it was no business of his, he went through the ceremony without further trouble.

Once more, let me thank you for your kind wishes, and with kind regards, I remain, dear Lady Gregory, very sincerely yours, Maud Gonne.

I am looking forward eagerly to the appearance of your new book on Finn, your Cuchulain is one of my husband's and my favourite books.

Back in Paris, she resumed her life of entertaining combined with propaganda; a journalist in June reported that "at her handsome apartments in the Avenue d'Eylau are to be seen deputies, journalists, and irreconcilables—men who have great power in the moulding of French opinion". If MacBride could not visit Dublin, she still could, and she was there to organise a protest against the first visit of the new monarch, more dangerous even than "old Vic" in her eyes because through him would be cemented the Entente Cordiale. A year later, in February of 1904, her son was born, and received the Irish version of his father's name, Sean.

A year later again, Yeats and her other Irish friends learned that she was seeking the civil dissolution of her marriage; as a Catholic she could not, of course, seek a divorce. MacBride contested the petition, and she was obliged to make public details of wrongs she would far rather have concealed. He had found life with the loveliest woman in Europe unendurable, her brilliance, her leadership, even her money exacerbating his sense of being on the scrap-heap. He drank, he knocked her about. It is possible to feel profoundly sorry for them both.

Yeats rushed over to Paris, and the extent of his generous suffering, as shown in his letters to Lady Gregory, moved and comforted Maud Gonne in her trouble, though characteristically she told him: "You must keep out of this, I've brought it on myself." The effect on the Nationalist movement was unfortunate, for MacBride was still a public figure and had many supporters. When next she was in Dublin, she, Kathleen ni Houlihan, was hissed by Nationalists at an Abbey first night.

The bad feeling blew over eventually, but with a curious and ironic dénouement when the legal complications were sorted out. MacBride was in the end able to return to Ireland, and she was not. She feared that if she were there for any length of time, he would succeed in obtaining custody of the child. She was therefore, except for an occasional flying visit, exiled from the scene of her every hope and thought for the next twelve years.

I 2

She was not unfitted for domesticity. Mademoiselle's admirable instruction had included the art of cookery, and although these were still the days of easily-found servants, and she never had any difficulty in securing their devotion, it was often her pleasure to prepare a special dish for a party, or create some exquisite sauce. She was a gifted amateur artist, and I have seen examples of her shell-flower work which suggest that she could have made a living that way had it been necessary. The amazing creature could truly have said, with the first Queen Elizabeth, "I am endued with such qualities that if I were turned out of the Realm in my petticoat, I were able to live in any place in Christome."

She moved into a smaller flat in the rue de Passy, and was able to create a more settled home for little Sean than any Iseult had known. But she did not dwindle into a mother, any more than she had dwindled into a wife. The letters of Yeats kept her faithfully in touch with Irish art and politics, and so did those of Helena Molony, who had become secretary of Inghinidhe when Mary Quinn married the actor Dudley Digges and went to America. Every week, Miss Molony recalls, she wrote a report to the President in Paris, and every year she spent a few days in the pretty flat and came back full of encouragement and inspiration.

The days of *L'Irlande Libre* were over, but Maud Gonne retained her faith in the power of the press, and presently she and Helena Molony decided to counter the frivolous and degrading effect of English women's magazines by starting a monthly of their own. *Bean na hEireann* (The Woman of Ireland) first appeared in 1908, with Helena Molony as editor, and with a heading of heroic female peasant figure, round tower and sunrise designed by a recent high-born recruit to the society, the Countess Markievicz.

Helena Molony smiles when she looks back on *Bean* now, but for all the amateurishness of its make-up and style, it holds in the not very distinguished annals of women's journalism a position heroic and unique. Fashion and beauty are used to gild the pill of revolutionary propaganda. A report beginning "How perfectly lovely are the hats this season . . ." rubs shoulders with a treatise on the art of street fighting: "The first thing is to break all the street lamps, leaving the district in total darkness. Then ropes and wires are stretched across the street . . ."

The gentleness of a serial by Katharine Tynan, and of poems by James Stephens and A. E., frames homilies on the use of physical force (unsigned, but one recognises the Countess's style): "Learn to discipline and be disciplined, learn to shoot, learn to march, learn to scout, learn to give up all for Ireland." The fair readers are reminded of Fenian sufferings, and encouraged by the thought that "the most we have to bear today is a few months in an English jail". In Madame Markievicz's gardening notes, instruction and propaganda are neatly combined: "A good Nationalist should look upon slugs in a garden much in the same way as she looks on the English in Ireland, and only regret that she cannot crush the Nation's enemies with the same ease that she can crush the garden's—with just one tread of her fairy foot."

"Our brothers may smile at such bloodthirsty sentiments in a woman's journal," says a rather defensive editorial, "but somebody must speak out, and *Bean na hEireann* offers no apology for being that one." By 1910 she was the only one, for Griffith's *Sinn Fein*, the other paper advocating physical force, had been suppressed, and *Bean* could justly claim to be "the ladies' paper that all the young men read". It carried articles by Griffith and Connolly, announcements of meetings in Beresford Place, the Nationalist stamping-ground behind the Custom House, labour notes, and reports of such minor triumphs as the sticking of an anti-enlistment label on the back of Lady Aberdeen's motor-car.

Maud Gonne's articles were mainly on the suffering of Irish working-class women and children, and she did not need to look far for her examples at a time when Dublin had the highest infant mortality rate in Europe. She could cite a stout-bottling factory where women worked a ten-hour day for 4s. 6d. weekly, or the common spectacle of children going to school breakfastless and not allowed a lunch-hour long enough to get home for a meal of tea-and-skim; she could attribute the high rate of adult lunacy and drunkenness to childhood under-nourishment.

France, England, Scotland and Wales had all made a start with school meals services, she told her readers; why was nothing being done in Ireland? And a few issues later, they learned that the School Dinner Committee of Inghinid-he had begun its work, and that 250 children at St. Auden's

School were being provided with a good dinner of Irish stew and rice pudding. The mothers who could pay gave a penny, so that there should be no taint of charity, and the rest got their dinners free. It was hoped that this school would serve as a model to the rest.

It may have been this venture which inspired Constance Markievicz to run her famous Liberty Hall canteen during the strikes and lock-outs of 1913. But Maud Gonne from her French exile was just as passionately on the side of the workers in their struggle against their grisly labour conditions. In November of 1913 she contributed a piece headed "The Real Criminals" to Jim Larkin's paper, *The Irish Worker*, in which she proclaimed that "because the workers have shown that poor and down-trodden as they are, their souls are not enslaved and they are worthy of Ireland, the employers have declared they will starve them into submission, and that their women and children shall die of hunger on the streets. In a free country employers of labour would never have dared to propose such a thing, for they would have been treated as the criminals they are. In Ireland they are protected by a police force over which Ireland has no control, and encouraged by a magistracy whose object seems to be to make justice a derision."

1913 was a year of new beginnings, and later in this same month the Irish Volunteers were formed, with an auxiliary women's force, to be known as the Cumann na mBan. As it was desirable to co-ordinate all the nationalist bodies, Inghinidhe decided to merge with Cumann na mBan, though at first retaining its identity as a separate branch.

Irish feminists, looking back now, are inclined to think that this was a pity, for though the Cumann did stalwart revolutionary work, it was by its constitution an auxiliary, and its members tended to be thought of as camp-followers. It never had quite the independence and flow of creative ideas that Inghinidhe na hEireann had displayed for thirteen years under the personal leadership of Maud Gonne.

13

For the children's sake she took a furnished house each summer at Colleville on the Normandy coast, and here from 1909 Yeats joined them for regular visits, which were not interrupted by the outbreak of war in 1914. This event seemed to her the inevitable outcome of the detested Entente Cordiale, and she was of course vehemently opposed to any Irish participation in it, and claimed to have had a vision of ruined houses in O'Connell Street. She took this to mean German bombing of Dublin, but in the light of later events decided it had been a premonition of the 1916 Rising. She did, however, modify her principles sufficiently to help in nursing the wounded in a French war hospital.

News of the Rising drove her wild with delight; she wrote to Yeats that "tragic destiny has returned to Ireland", and devoured the newspapers he sent her every day. The tragic destiny played itself out; the leaders faced the British firing squads, and she was a widow. John MacBride had been eking out an obscure livelihood as a minor official of the Dublin Waterworks, and taking no part in politics, but the call to arms roused him to the one thing he could do supremely well. He fought gallantly, faced his court martial with dignity, and died a hero's death.

It cannot be supposed that she mourned him. Her grief was for the leaders who had shown constructive, down-to-earth, Socialist ideas, and particularly for Connolly, whose outstanding ability she had recognised almost from the start of his career. She knew that his loss was irretrievable. Tom Clarke's death was another personal blow; he had been the last and staunchest of the Treason Felony prisoners, not released till 1898.

Her only thought was to get back to Ireland, and work for the families of the prisoners and the dead. What she needed from Yeats when he came over in the summer was his help in getting her a passport, not the final proposal of marriage which he felt himself bound in honour to make. For the first time, her refusal was received by him with relief.

For the fates had played a knavish trick on the poet. Maud Gonne's children were growing up, Sean into a clever school-boy, who, Yeats reported to Lady Gregory, "to my amusement has begun to criticise his mother's politics, he has a confident analytical mind and is more like a boy of 17 than 13", Iseult into a poignant reminder of her mother's looks when young. He fancied himself in love with the girl, and confided his hopes to Maud, who said that she would not stand in his way, but that she doubted if Iseult would take him seriously.

And so it proved. Iseult was flattered, kept him dangling, then declined, though she was genuinely fond of him, and made him her confidant in her subsequent matrimonial troubles. Freed at last from the Gonne thrall, Yeats had the good fortune to marry a young woman of independent intelligence who was prepared to absorb herself in his con-cerns, and under whose influence his finest work was still to be written.

The anniversary of the Rising passed, and the only crumb of comfort was Helena Molony's report of how she and other Inghinidhe stalwarts had hung tricolor flags out over the Post Office and the College of Surgeons, and had reprinted the Proclamation of Independence and pasted it on pillar-boxes all over the city. ("It took the police and fire brigade hours to get the Post Office flag down," Helena Molony recalls, "and as for the Proclamations, we'd used glue with the paste and fairly enamelled them on. They were there for weeks.")

At length Yeats secured the passports, and the little family pulled up its French roots and came to London in the autumn of 1917. Under the Defence of the Realm Act, Maud was refused permission to proceed to Ireland, but she disguised herself as a fat old woman by stuffing her clothes with cushions and hoodwinked the officials. This time, she rented a house at 73 Stephens Green.

The Dublin to which she returned was not the city of her youth; it had been steeled to the true temper of revolution not so much by the Rising as by the brutal stupidity of the reprisals. The survivors returned from their English gaols with prestige immeasurably enhanced, and there took place a great re-welding of forces under the general title of Sinn Fein, and under the new leader, Eamonn de Valera, in whose favour her old friend Arthur Griffith stood down. Beside these professionals she was an amateur, and had the wit to recognise it. She took no part in their deliberations. Her function was, as always, to symbolise and to inspire.

She was still the most striking looking person in any gathering, and from this time on she wore widow's weeds, with a headdress and flowing black veil on the French model. She was in mourning for Ireland, she was careful to explain, and not for MacBride. Blatant self-advertisement, her opponents sneered; from this distance it looks more like inspired common sense. Perhaps she had another of her "visions" and foresaw the skimpy fashions of the later 1920's. The flamboyant modes of the late Victorian and Edwardian periods might have been designed for her splendid stature, but the cloche hat and knee-length skirt would have made her look ridiculous.

At all events, she must have symbolised to good effect, for when a "German plot" was fabricated by the Government in May 1918 as a pretext for getting the Sinn Fein leaders under lock and key, she was considered sufficiently dangerous to share the honour of arrest and deportation with Constance Markievicz and Tom Clarke's widow Kathleen. An entire landing in Holloway Gaol was cleared for the three "wild Irishwomen", and the nightmare of the prisoner's lot, which had haunted her throughout her political life, became at last her own.

c

14

They were not officially prisoners, only internees, as they had stood no trial, but at first conditions were much the same. They were locked up, in darkness, for twelve hours every night, and only allowed an hour's exercise at midday. They protested, and gradually secured improvements. As internees they could have meals sent in by paying for them, and Constance, the experienced old lag, took advantage of the concession. But Maud Gonne and Kathleen Clarke maintained that the Government which was holding them without trial had the duty of feeding them, and their health deteriorated rapidly on a diet of milkless cocoa and starch.

They were racked with anxiety about their young sons; "I think of my companions as Niobe and Rachel" commented Constance in a letter to her sister Eva. And an aggravation of their plight was that they were completely isolated. An undertaking had been demanded, not to talk politics with visitors, or to pass on to visitors political messages or reports. In the face of this further, and monstrous, infringement of their civil rights, they very properly refused visitors altogether.

Constance Markievicz and Kathleen Clarke settled down to make the best of it, with books and painting, and with embroidery, for which they used the canopies of the deck-chairs sent in by Eva as frames. But Maud Gonne could not endure to be shut up.

"All she'd do was talk to her canary in a cage," Mrs. Clarke recalls. "She was like a caged wild animal herself, like a tigress prowling endlessly up and down. We were given the chance to apply to the Sankey Commission for release, and in her misery she said she would—said she'd point out that she hadn't been in Ireland during the war. Con said: "If you do that, you need never come back to Ireland," and she tore the application up. After that she fell sick, or maybe feigned sick, she was such a good actress that you couldn't tell." Constance's letters suggest that her illness was real enough, even if psychosomatic. At any rate, they were eventually all three transferred to the hospital wing, where conditions were more endurable.

The deaths of two people who had been close to her added to Maud's depression, first her beautiful gentle sister Kathleen, and then Millevoye. He had become an active political opponent, a Clemenceau henchman and supporter of the Entente; nevertheless he was the only man who had touched her heart, and she might well feel that he should have died hereafter.

Yeats in the meantime, while pulling every string to secure her release, was living in her Stephens Green house, which she had lent to him in order that his first child might be born on Irish soil. After six months of internment she was removed to a sanatorium, and from this she efficiently escaped, disguised as a nurse, and boarded the Irish Mail at Euston. Next morning she knocked on the door of her house, expecting to be taken in, but Yeats, in view of the fact that his wife was not only pregnant but convalescent after influenza, refused, and there was a stormy scene.

But however much they might disagree over politics, there was too close a link between the friends for permanent ill-will. The Yeatses moved out into lodgings, and the Chief Secretary did not interfere further with Maud, who was able to resume her life of political hostess at Number 73. She was still a superb party-giver, and those who met the poet at her parties observed that she treated him with her old easy camaraderie, and that he, for all his fame and growing aloofness, would always go out of his way to do a kindness to anyone who was a friend of Maud Gonne.

15

Her chief work during the Black and Tan war was with the White Cross, an organisation which Griffith had asked the women of Ireland to set up for the relief of victims and their dependents. The bulk of its funds were collected in America, and shiploads of food were sent over and distributed. This was the sort of work she loved—rebuilding the homes of those who had had their roofs burnt over their heads, keeping prisoners' children fed and clothed, organising her speciality of school dinners. She left to professionals like Constance Markievicz the struggle to build the infant Dail Eireann into an effective Parliament of Ireland. When Constance was gaoled again in Cork in the summer of 1919, Maud Gonne visited her with a bouquet containing an automatic—a gesture fairly common among those visiting prisons at the period. The pistol was, however, intercepted by the authorities, and Constance remained in gaol.

A new friend was Mrs. Despard, an elderly woman whose advanced left-wing views gained further piquancy from the fact that she was the sister of the Viceroy, French of Ypres, and a sad thorn in his flesh. She was a frequent visitor to 73 Stephens Green, and eventually made it her home.

No one was to be a bitterer opponent than Maud Gonne of the Treaty which ended the war with England and betrayed, as the Republicans felt, all they had fought for, but at the time of its signing in December 1921 she seems to have acquiesced. She was, after all, a lifelong friend of Griffith, who had had the ungrateful task of leading the treaty delegation to London, and she had no particular attachment to President de Valera, who had stayed at home and then disowned his delegation's work. De Valera resigned, Griffith took over the Presidency, and Maud was in his confidence to the extent that he used her as a kind of unofficial envoy to the French. She was in Paris, on a Government mission to protest about Orange murders of Catholics, when news reached her that the Republican rebels who had occupied the Four Courts in Dublin were being shelled.

She rushed home, and saw the Lord Mayor, who asked her to get together "some of the women who are not afraid and who want peace". A delegation consisting of herself, Mrs. Despard, the suffragette leader Mrs. Sheehy-Skeffington, and others was on the point of leaving for the Four Courts when the surrender was announced. It then divided into two groups, one, including herself, calling on Griffith, Collins and Cosgrave, the other on the Republicans, with proposals for an immediate cessation of hostilities throughout the country until the Dail could meet on July 2nd, a truce, and no arrests.

The Republicans agreed, but the Government, who rather naturally regarded the defenders of the Four Courts as rebels against their democratically elected rulers, did not, and sent the women's delegation a message to that effect. Maud Gonne clamoured to see Griffith in person. He came to the door of the Council Chamber and gave her a curt answer: "We are now a Government and we have to keep order." The two old friends did not meet again.

She went home filled with disquiet over Griffith's policy, and his death from anxiety and overwork next month left her without emotional attachment to his side, soon to become the officially recognised Irish Free State. The Four Courts leaders were held as hostages for Republican good behaviour, and when in December a Free State Deputy was shot dead in a Dublin street, four of them were executed as a reprisal. Maud Gonne's disillusionment was complete, and henceforward the Cosgrave Government were in her eyes the archfiends, worse even than the British, betrayers of their own people.

The Free State constitution provided for an upper house, and one of the first nominated Senators was Yeats. To his literary friends it was the fitting recognition of a career which had done so much to "bring back dignity to Ireland", but to Maud Gonne it was the ultimate apostasy. "We quarrelled seriously", she wrote in *Scattering Branches*, "when he became a Senator of a Free State which voted Flogging Acts against young Republican soldiers seeking to free Ireland from the contamination of the British Empire, and for several years we ceased to meet."

16

She had always liked country life, and in 1922 she and Mrs. Despard moved out to Roebuck House, a pleasantly spacious Victorian mansion between the city and the mountains, surrounded by fields where their menagerie of dogs and other pets could run free. Here they set up jam-making and shell-flower factories to give employment to the dependants of Republicans killed or taken prisoner in the Civil War, and from here they organised their Women's Prisoners' Defence League. Every Sunday, week after week, their black-robed figures headed a procession of women demonstrating on "the ruins corner" in O'Connell Street, where the shelling of 1916 had reduced the Gresham Hotel to rubble.

The W.P.D.L. collected food and clothing for prisoners, arranged for visits from relatives, conducted processions of their children to various churches to pray for their release, and did all these things in the most flamboyant manner possible, giving the Cosgrave Government no peace. Nothing could happen to prisoners without their hearing of it, and, by means of poster parades, informing the outside world.

Finally the Government lost patience, and Maud was arrested. Her second taste of imprisonment was at Kilmainham, in January of 1923. This time she went immediately on hunger-strike, and Mrs. Despard and the other supporters maintained a ceaseless vigil outside the gaol. Poor Yeats, repudiated but ever-faithful, appealed to Mr. Cosgrave, who replied gloomily that women ought to keep out of politics. But it would have been awkward for any Irish Government to let Maud Gonne die. After twenty days she was released, and carried out on a stretcher amid the cheers of a large crowd. In the autumn, all the Republican prisoners went on hunger-strike, and the Defence League opened a convalescent home in Harcourt Street for those who "crawled out more dead than alive".

There were repeated police attempts to ban the League, but it would bob up again under another name; likewise to proscribe its meetings, but Maud Gonne produced a portable platform and held impromptu ones in places where they were least expected. "We had the police running all over the country", a supporter recalls. Finally the authorities gave up; as Maud put it, "I expect they said, those damned women make more trouble than the meetings are worth."

But if some Dublin cynics agreed, the stories of her courage and magnetism in these years show that she still held the popular imagination. R. M. Fox was an eyewitness of the great demonstration in O'Connell Street after the murder of Kevin O'Higgins and the arrest of Republican suspects. The police had forbidden the gathering of crowds in the streets, but they came nevertheless, and through them Maud Gonne "slowly advanced, leading her Defence League women, carrying a huge bouquet of flowers and looking radiant. In some strange fashion her presence filled that great audience with a sense of irresistible power." Or again, there was the demonstration outside General Mulcahy's house, when soldiers had fired over the crowd's heads, and she climbed up on to a parapet and stared smiling for a full minute at the young officer in charge; the order to fire was not given.

The return to power of de Valera in 1932 found her guarded; she waited to see how he would turn out, and in due course was disappointed. The Republican leader proved just as tough with the physical force wing of his own party as his predecessor had been. Once more she campaigned for young gunmen who were giving their lives to end Partition, or were just plain gangsters, according to your political viewpoint. Yeats, whom she now saw occasionally, could not withhold his admiration from such unquenchable, incorrigible vitality. He too had a house in the Dublin suburbs, and their last meeting, an affectionate one, took place there in the late summer of 1938. Then he went abroad, to be caught by the war and die far from home.

Scattering Branches, a collection of tributes to the poet by his friends, was published in 1940, and she wrote the chapter on "Yeats and Ireland". It is a generous appreciation, granting to him more political significance than perhaps she had given him in his lifetime. She concedes that without him there would have been no literary movement, and that without the inspiration of the literary movement there might not have been an Easter Week. "He is gone," she concludes, "and I am the prisoner of old age, waiting for release. The Ireland I live in is very different from the Ireland of our dream, because our dream is not yet achieved."

She says nothing of his love for her, or of the great poetry inspired by it, and this is not only *comme il faut* but also, I think, significant. For although she had earlier paid lip-service to his poetry, I doubt if she really considered it important. While people were starving, or being evicted, or languishing in English prisons, the writing of love-lyrics appeared to her just so much waste of time. In her eyes Willie was the author of one supreme work, and it was very tiresome of him, having proved that he could do it, to spend the rest of his career steadfastly refusing to do it again.

17

She parted company amicably with Mrs. Despard when
the latter's politics veered further to the left than even she
could countenance, but her son and his wife made their home
with her, and she had the happiness of watching a grandson
and granddaughter grow up, and Sean MacBride's career
develop brilliantly as barrister and as statesman. Partition
was a burning question with them both, and in the late
1930's she helped him form his own party, the Clann na
Poblachte, which took a much tougher stand on Partition
than de Valera's Fianna Fail, and aimed at sending deputies
to the Dail while preserving good relations with the banned
I.R.A. It contended that the *raison d'être* of this rebel force
would not disappear until a true Republic of thirty-two
counties had been realised.

Maud Gonne published her memoirs, *A Servant of the
Queen*, in 1938, and even by the standards of a country whose
every second citizen seems to have it in him to write a good
autobiography, hers is exceptionally racy and dramatic.
Dates may be suspect, chronology scarcely exists, but the
entertainment is unflagging. One hears her very voice, and it
is the voice of a rebellious girl, never of a septuagenarian.
Of course she is violently partisan, sometimes unfair, occasionally (as in her account of Lady Gregory) malicious.
But as always, she is irresistible. The story ends with her
marriage, and she promises a second volume, but it does not
seem to have got beyond the stage of discussion.

The I.R.A.'s campaign of violence in England during the
Second World War was not countenanced by Sean Mac-
Bride. Nevertheless, his mother could not altogether harden

her heart against these young men who were still trying to make England's difficulty Ireland's opportunity, and she was active in movements for the reprieve of those sentenced to death, maintaining that the real responsibility lay with the two major parties, for their abandonment of republican aims.

But these last years were disheartening, and the plight of prisoners generally, rather than of specific political prisoners, came to absorb more of her attention. To the end of her life she continued to call for drastic changes in the Irish prison system, particularly as it affected women and children. When she broke her leg as the result of a fall and had an hour to wait for the ambulance, she passed the time in drafting yet another memorandum on the subject of prison reform.

She was old and grey, but not, as her poet had prophesied, full of sleep. She raged at her ageing body. "It's so awful to be old," was her continual cry, "and not able to *do* anything." The reigning generation of Dublin wits and writers, men like Micheal MacLiammoir, Monk Gibbon and Roger MacHugh, could talk to her as to a contemporary. Mr. MacLiammoir catches her in a moment of repose: "her heroic and now cavernous beauty, made sombre by the customary black draperies she wore, was also illumined by an increasing gentleness and humour; she had what now seemed a faint far-away amusement at life." But let any case of oppression or injustice come to her ears, and out again would leap the young lioness, tawny and terrible.

With the Costello Coalition Government of 1948, her son at last attained the position for which his abilities and his European education eminently fitted him, and even those who disagree with his domestic policies usually concede that he was the best Minister for External Affairs that Ireland has yet known. His two years of office were a fitting crown to her old age, and in them he was mainly responsible for Costello's repeal of the External Relations Act, which severed the last link with Britain. The twenty-six counties became a Republic, and part of his mother's political ambition was achieved, though of course she could never be satisfied while Partition remained. It was Sean MacBride, fittingly, who represented the Government when Yeats's body was brought back from France and re-interred in Drumcliffe churchyard in September of 1948.

She was ailing for the last six months of her long life, devotedly nursed by her daughter-in-law, and bearing her illness with a patience which astonished those who had seen her fury over the broken leg. She was tired at last, and ready to go. She died on April 27th, 1953, and was buried two days later in the Republican Plot in Glasnevin cemetery. The Dubliners gave her one of those fine political funerals in which they specialise, and it was attended by Mr. de Valera, whom she had so often criticised, and most of his government. Her coffin draped in the national flag was carried in procession through the city, watched by thousands, and in Westmorland Street big groups of old I.R.A. men and Cumann na mBan women fell silently in behind it.

Although crowds gathered once if she but showed her face . . . There was no "once" about it. They gathered still.

18

Although crowds gathered once if she but showed her face
And even old men's eyes grew dim, this hand alone,
Like some last courtier at a gypsy camping-place,
Babbling of fallen majesty, records what's gone.

That is Yeats at his most splendid, hammering out his thought in bronze. But does it embody the whole truth? Will she only be remembered as Laura and Beatrice are remembered, faceless women, Muses and no more?

I cannot think so. Ireland forgets much in her history, but never the myth, the symbol, the banner, and Maud Gonne was all that. She was also enormously a person in her own right, vital, generous, flamboyant, brave. She had her faults and I hope I have not minimised them, but those who saw in her the Irish Joan of Arc were not without some justification. It was fortunate for her person, but less lucky for her fame, that we English no longer burned our enemies at the stake.

It is to Yeats's credit that he loved her "because of that great nobleness of hers"; not just because she was beautiful, but because her beauty meant joy and freedom. He says so, over and over again, and there is no doubting the sincerity of his youth and middle age. He criticised her too, but on the whole fairly; he was right to deplore her insensitivity to literature, her wilful blindness over the incompatibility of propaganda and art.

But towards the end of his life, though his personal loyalty to her did not waver, his poetic attitude underwent a change. Stripped of the splendid language, the sentiment boils down to: such a pity Maud had to waste her beauty on those ugly politics, instead of preserving it for man's delectation. The very qualities which had inspired him are now rejected and denied. He wishes to make her what she could so easily have been; what almost any other woman with her looks, born at her period, would have been; an odalisque.

And because his later verse is now seen as his most important, biographers and commentators all tend to agree with this view of Maud Gonne. (It is excellently summarised in *Images of a Poet*, the *catalogue raisonné* of the Yeats iconography made by Professor D. J. Gordon and Mr. Ian Fletcher in 1961.)

But she did not waste her beauty, she spent it, and like all gifts spent in a good cause it returned to her tenfold. She used it as one of her weapons in a long, fighting life, which brought trouble to a few, but benefit to many. In particular, she put new heart into the women of Ireland. Had it not been for her arrival on the scene in 1888, they would probably have taken a much smaller and less spirited part in the liberation movement. She taught them to campaign and agitate, and not be afraid of the sound of their own voices, and she also showed them the way to works of social service—let not her school dinners be forgotten. She was always, and passionately, on the side of the under-dog. The hungry family in the Dublin tenement, the evicted family on the cold hillside would never let her rest.

There is a choice of noble lines for her epitaph: I choose the couplet, not so often quoted as some, which seems to me to come closest to the truth:

Though she had young men's praise and old men's blame,
Among the poor both old and young gave her praise.

SOURCES:

Maud Gonne MacBride: *A Servant of the Queen*. London, Gollancz, 1938.
W. B. Yeats: *The Trembling of the Veil*. London, Laurie, 1922.
—— *Letters*, edited by Allan Wade. London, Hart-Davis, 1954.
Joseph Hone: *W. B. Yeats, 1865–1939*. London, Macmillan, 1942.
Katharine Tynan: *Twenty-Five Years: Reminiscences*. London, Smith, Elder, 1913.
Stephen Gwynn, ed.: *Scattering Branches: Tributes to the Memory of W. B. Yeats*. London, Macmillan, 1940. (Contains an essay on Yeats by Maud Gonne.)
Files of *The United Irishman, Bean na hEireann*, and *The Gael*.
Henderson Scrapbook of the Abbey Theatre, National Library of Ireland.

Recollections of Mrs. Sean MacBride, Dr. Roger MacHugh, Mr. Ian Stuart, Mrs. Tom Clarke, Miss Helena Molony, "John Brennan" (Mrs. Czira).

Constance Markievicz

I

IT IS not true that Constance Markievicz has been forgotten; her name is too tightly built into Ireland's history, and even England's, for that. But her legend, even more than Maud Gonne's, has been distorted. She is remembered for the wrong reasons, in the wrong way.

In England, as "the Red Countess", a baleful figure with a sinister foreign name, advocate of rebellion and murder; a stumbling-block, moreover, to young journalists, who must always qualify a description of Lady Astor as "the first woman Member of Parliament" with the words "to take her seat".

In Ireland, as a national heroine, the only one in Dublin to be honoured with a statue (a singularly unconvincing and prettified bust among the flower-beds in Stephens Green). But beneath the lip-service, regarded with a curious ambivalence, accused of undue fanaticism and bitterness, blamed for much that was not her fault. She was upper-class and almost English, people will tell you; her voice was shrill and strident; of course she fought bravely alongside the men in the Rising, but is it really a woman's place to put on uniform and shoot to kill? Maud Gonne, yes, she was so lovely and gracious you'd forgive her anything. But Constance Markievicz, no; hers is not the image of Irish womanhood we want to present to the outside world.

The crude, charmless, virago-picture almost imposes itself —and then one meets one of her comrades in arms, or comes across the slangy, impetuous letters she wrote to her sister during her many imprisonments, and it is like coming out of a dark tunnel into the strong sweet air of her own west coast. Wrong-headed she was sometimes, tactless often, lacking in that easy charm of manner which is so usual in Ireland that to be without it seems almost an indecency. But a splendid, generous, strong-hearted creature, genuinely one of those to whom the miseries of the world are misery, and will not let them rest.

She was born Constance Georgina Gore-Booth, of a great West of Ireland family, the Gore-Booths of Lissadell, ten miles north of Sligo. It is customary to speak of her as a rebel against her class, but most of the Gore-Booths displayed strong social consciences, and there was a streak of eccentricity in them. Her father was an enlightened landlord who had kept his tenants alive through the famine years, her mother started home industries to help them, and the heir, her brother Joscelyn, was to become a leading figure in the co-operative creamery movement.

"A very pleasant, kindly, inflammable family", Yeats wrote of them after his first visit to Lissadell in the autumn of 1894. "Ever ready to take up new ideas and new things. The eldest son is 'theoretically' a home ruler and practically some kind of a humanitarian, much troubled by the responsibility of his wealth and almost painfully conscientious." Constance was the first-born (February 4th, 1868), then came Joscelyn, then Eva, the dearest to her of the family. The Gore-Booths were a united clan, and they stuck by Constance through all her troubles, when in the eyes of most of her class she was irretrievably disgraced.

The beauty of Constance and Eva as children, and their fearless horsemanship, are still legendary in Sligo. They were inadequately governess-educated, being in that no worse off than most young ladies in the Ireland of their day. Nobody could foresee that Eva would have a serious poetic gift, and that Constance would share in the government of her country, and that the lack of early mental discipline would prove a drawback to them both.

Writing years afterwards in a revolutionary newspaper, Constance gives a lyrical picture of her childhood. "We lived on a beautiful, enchanted West Coast, where we grew up intimate with the soft mists and the coloured mountains, and where each morning you woke to the sound of the wild birds. . . . No one was interested in politics in our house. Irish history also was taboo, for 'what is the use of brooding on past grievances?'" But the two girls observed the landlord class in their big demesnes, and the prosperous Protestant farmers with Scottish names, "while hidden away among rocks on the bleak mountain sides, or soaking in the slime and ooze of the boglands, or beside the Atlantic shore where the grass is blasted yellow by the salt west wind, you find the dispossessed people of the old Gaelic race in their miserable cabins."

They did what they could to help their poorer neighbours, were constant and welcome visitors to the cottages, were adored by the house servants. The son of a stud-groom at Lissadell told Katharine Tynan, years afterwards, how Miss Constance had sat up with his father night after night, nursing him through a dangerous illness, and how she had found his mother near her confinement washing clothes, and put her away from the tub and finished the washing herself. But on the social system which permitted these glaring inequalities between rich and poor, they did not reflect. As Constance puts it: "though Irish in all one's inmost feelings, one's superficial outlook was aloof and vague."

Eva wrote poems; painting and woodcarving, for which she supposed herself to have a talent, were Constance's creative outlet. She had a passion for amateur theatricals, too, and though she was too self-conscious to make a good actress, early showed a gift for disguise. A judge of assize, staying at Lissadell, declared one evening at dinner that no disguise could deceive him, and on his way to court next day, found a peasant cart overturned in the road and a young mother and baby weeping beside it. He stopped his carriage, and while his groom righted the cart, he comforted the young woman with the gift of a sovereign. Miss Constance returned him his sovereign that evening.

Photographs of the sisters in their debutante days show a very great beauty, and seasons in London produced for them many admirers, but no one to hold their interest. It was a holiday in Italy that enabled Eva to escape from the gilded cage. She met her lifelong friend, Esther Roper, already working for women's suffrage and to better the conditions of the Lancashire mill-girls; and presently joined her in Manchester in a twenty-seven years' partnership, striving not towards "some vague Utopia", as Yeats put it in a lovely and libellous poem, but towards a decent standard of life for women in industry, and their recognition by the trade union movement, which had hitherto largely ignored them.

Among Eva's early crusades was one to organise barmaids, when attempts were made to banish them on alleged moral grounds. Women circus performers and flower-sellers were others who, thanks largely to her, were not deprived of the right to work. And the appearance of an organised force of women textile workers, the creation of Esther Roper and Eva Gore-Booth, was probably the biggest single factor in rearousing interest in women's suffrage in the early years of the century. When Yeats criticised Eva's poetry as formless and insufficiently disciplined, he was speaking of what he understood. But when he wrote of her as one who wasted youth and beauty in "the folly of a fight", he merely proved that he could no more appreciate her true quality than he did that of Constance—or even of Maud Gonne.

2

Dissatisfied with the life of hunting and parties at Lissadell, Constance clung to the belief that she might become a painter. She took a course at the Slade, then in 1898 went to Paris to study at Julien's. There she met Casimir Markievicz, a Polish widower, younger than herself and with a baby son. Marriage to a foreigner, even a titled one, could hardly have been what the Gore-Booths hoped for their brilliant eldest child. But as usual they put a good face on her doings, and gave her a society wedding in London. And as Casimir did not appear likely to be a provider, they also set her up in a comfortable home in the suburbs of Dublin, Surrey House, Rathmines, and filled it with the beautiful furniture and ornaments that befitted the artist daughter of a great family.

And Cassie proved to be hardly a foreigner after all. It is generally agreed that he was an utterly charming creature who rapidly became more Irish than the Irish; Padraic Colum called him the only stage Irishman he had ever met. He had real talent as a painter, when he could be bothered to exercise it, but he slipped into the social life of Dublin like a goldfish into a well-tended pool, and like so many other talented people in that beguiling city, soon preferred talking and drinking to any other way of passing the time.

"The Gore-Booth girl who married the Polish count with the unspellable name is going to settle near Dublin," wrote A. E. to Sarah Purser, "and as they are both clever it will help to create an art atmosphere. We might get the materials for a revolt, a new Irish Art Club. I feel some desperate schism or earthquaking revolution is required to

wake up Dublin in art matters." There were certainly the
materials for a revolt in Constance, but it was not to be of the
artistic kind.

She loved her Cassie dearly, and also her little stepson,
Stanislaus. She loved—but less dearly, since she had always
preferred boys to girls—the daughter born to them after a
year of marriage, and christened Maeve after the warrior
queen who is reputedly buried on the mountain-top above
Lissadell. But Cassie, she soon realised, was a lightweight.
Being married to him was not a full-time occupation. The
children could be left to nurses and governesses, and given
ever-longer holidays at Lissadell. Meanwhile, she had under
her eyes and nose much worse evidence of poverty and
exploitation than ever she had encountered on the bogs and
salt-flats of the west.

A bundle of old newspapers, back copies of W. P. Ryan's
Irish Peasant and Griffith's *Sinn Fein*, first, she says, opened her
eyes to the possibility of political action. At A. E.'s, she met
Griffith himself, and then Helena Molony, Maud Gonne's
lieutenant, who introduced her to Inghinidhe na hEireann.

It was in 1908. She was forty, a wife and mother, and a
well-known artistic hostess. But the real purpose of her life
was only now beginning.

3

The Daughters of Erin were at first understandably
suspicious of this society woman come slumming among
them. Some even suggested that she might be a spy from the
vice-regal court. They were repelled by her high, clear and to
them English-sounding voice, and by the habit of command
which comes naturally to a daughter of the Great House.

But her sincerity and genuine longing to be of service soon won them over. "She was like a twelve-year-old boy, boisterous and noisy, coming bouncing in with her dogs," Helena Molony affectionately recalls.

They first gave her work organising girls' dramatic classes, but girls bored her, and she moved on to a more successful class for boys. It was also about this time that she relegated Maeve entirely to the care of a devoted grandmother and governess. The governess, Miss Clayton, remembers how the Markieviczes would descend on Lissadell for the summer holidays, and the Countess would romp and quarrel like an elder sister with the fiery little girl who so closely resembled her, then depart as suddenly as she had come, leaving the child to mutter rather bitterly: "Well, that's over, she won't think of me for another year." Decidedly, Constance had not the maternal gift, and if challenged she could have answered that her child had every advantage, and that she was devoting herself to children who had almost none. But in Ireland, that temple of motherhood, it is another of the black marks set against her name.

By 1909 she was on the council of Sinn Fein, which under Griffith's guidance was a pacifist movement, with a negative, anti-recruiting military policy and no provision for organising forces of its own. The cleavage of view between her and Griffith rapidly widened: "we never became close friends," she says, "for I never thoroughly trusted and understood him and often disliked his methods." In the previous year Baden-Powell had founded the Boy Scout movement, and she heard with indignation that the Dublin Scouts had paraded before "the English Viceroy". Her success with the boys' classes in Inghinidhe suggested the possibility of founding a Nationalist scout brigade.

But "when I suggested that they should introduce into the Sinn Fein programme the formation of a rebel Boy Scout organisation, with the openly avowed purpose of laying the foundations of an Irish army to fight for freedom, the idea was not met with the enthusiasm which I, in my innocence, had expected."

With Helena Molony's help she went ahead nevertheless, and found better support from Jim Larkin, the trade union organiser, whose notion that Irish Labour should not be controlled from England filled her with delight. He was "some great primaeval force rather than a man", she pronounced. He let her use a room in his Irish Transport and General Workers' Union office as a Boy Scout headquarters, till she was able to find her own in the Camden Street Hall. She christened her body the Fianna, after Finn's legendary warrior band, and both its programme and her personality made an instant appeal. Adults she might annoy, but boys recognised her as one of themselves.

There was little space in the programme for woodcraft and the rest of the innocuous Baden-Powell skills. Instead, there were elementary foot-drill, route marches, signalling, first-aid, and the use of real firearms. The law permitted the use of guns on private property, and she rented a cottage in the Dublin mountains for two shillings a week, and took her boys out there at weekends. Schoolteacher friends helped with the rest of the work, but the arms training was her personal responsibility, and she took it very seriously. Boys who larked about with their guns were told that they were not worthy to carry one for Ireland.

The movement grew, new branches were formed, and Larkin allotted one of them a room in his newly completed headquarters, Liberty Hall. Then Constance conceived the grandiose plan of taking a country house with seven acres of ground, and using it both for military training, and as the home of a co-operative community with republican ideals. She had bitten off more than she could chew, and after various near-farcical disasters was glad to fall back on the suburban haven of Surrey House. But it was a lesson learnt; enthusiasm had to be backed by hard organisational work. Next time history offered her a chance, she made no mistake.

Dublin's horrible social and industrial conditions, and the attempts of the employers to break the rapidly growing power of the unions, built up into the explosive situation of 1913, when strikes and lock-outs between them threw some 24,000 people out of work. Constance flung herself upon the basement of Liberty Hall (a characteristic anecdote describes her snatching the scrubbing-brush from the solitary charwoman she found there, and crying "No one scrubs a floor as well as I do!") and organised a food kitchen and milk depot. For six months she worked day and night, collecting the funds, cooking the food, visiting the sick in their homes, and recruiting a band of helpers from all classes—for the work of mercy attracted people like her friends the Sheehy-Skeffingtons, who had no serious rebel leanings, but were revolted by the callousness shown on the employers' side. The Liberty Hall kitchen saved hundreds of children, and probably a good many of their parents, from actual death by starvation, and there are those who account it the finest achievement of Constance's life.

Surrey House, its carpets rolled up, its ornaments put away, became the home of countless casualties in this industrial war, and the unofficial address of Jim Larkin and his second-in-command, James Connolly, when they raised their Irish Citizen Army from among the strikers. The strike was finally broken, but the moral victory was with the workers, and the Citizen Army continued in being. Alongside it was another new body, the Irish Volunteers, formed as a reply to Ulster's arming across the border, and with a more widely based membership than the I.C.A. There was a certain rivalry between the two rebel bands, and the fact that the Countess was a member of both was strongly objected to by the secretary of the I.C.A., one Sean O'Casey, who eventually resigned on that account. In his *Story of the Irish Citizen Army*, the future playwright describes this affair in characteristically amusing and pugnacious detail.

Larkin and Connolly: these were the men whom

Constance loved, the two who seemed to her to have the root of the matter in them. Like Maud Gonne before her, she had little use for the poetic, Celtic-twilit side of the movement, but she responded instantly to the seasoned fighters from the working class, whose knowledge of its sufferings was bred in the bone, and in whose philosophy the Nationalist cause was indissolubly bound up with social revolution.

She was on the receiving end in the Howth gun-runnings, some of the arms being hidden at her mountain cottage. And if the outbreak of war in August 1914 split the Irish Volunteers and sent the majority of them into the British armed forces, the true revolutionary Nationalists, Constance among them, were in no way deflected from their aim, and began to make positive plans for turning England's difficulty into Ireland's opportunity.

Casimir Markievicz, however, went off to join the Polish Army, and to fight bravely for his native soil.

It was the end of a marriage which had been so gradually disintegrating that Constance herself seems hardly to have noticed. Cassie had endured her political activities with his usual good humour, and in the first years had shared in them to the extent of helping her write propaganda plays, and put them on with an amateur company when the Abbey stage could be borrowed for the purpose. But he had resented the Fianna, disapproved of the co-operative community, and ceased to find either privacy or comfort in his home. It was increasingly evident that his wife, though full of goodwill towards him and their children, had no time to spare for them.

Eventually, he consoled himself elsewhere, but she never did. She remained fond of him, and proud to bear his "unspellable" name. When in years to come he would pay a rare visit to Dublin, she welcomed him with a childlike excitement and pleasure—and forgot him as soon as he had left again. It was much the same attitude that she showed to Maeve. They were both summoned in her last illness, and she was happy to have them beside her as she died.

4

Eva Gore-Booth and Esther Roper, watching Constance's progress with sisterly anxiety from England, discounted the possibility of a Rising. They knew that she spent half her days and nights drilling and route marching, either with her Fianna boys, or with the re-formed Irish Citizen Army, of which she was joint treasurer. They were aware that Surrey House had become a quasi-military headquarters, and that its hostess never knew till breakfast next morning how many her roof had sheltered the night before. But when they visited Dublin, and saw a parade of the entire Nationalist forces—Citizen Army, Volunteers, Cumann na mBan, Fianna, and fellow-travellers—the total muster seemed to them so tiny, after the endless khaki lines on their way to the Front at home, that they looked at each other with relief and said: "Thank goodness, they can't be planning anything serious with *that*."

And even if they doubted Constance's practical sense, there was no mistaking that of James Connolly, who seemed to them both level-headed and humane, and who in discussion gave it as his view that armed risings were out of date. They were reassured, and Constance did not undeceive them. She knew that they were pacifist, opposed on principle to violent methods, and she wished to spare them as long as she could.

But a Rising had been decided on, quite early in the war; how could it have been otherwise? England was never likely to face a worse "difficulty" than this murderous war with Germany, and if the mass of the Irish people were not revolutionary, most of them having indeed relatives in the

British forces, still it is the general experience that revolutions are not made by the masses, but by resolute minorities. It is enough that the masses shall afterwards acquiesce. The bitterness of those who had suffered in the strikes and lock-outs was not assuaged because their sons had put on khaki, often enough as an alternative to starving at home. There was reason to suppose that the Irish masses would acquiesce; and after all, the fact that the climate of opinion changed radically within a year of the Easter Rising suggests that this calculation was not altogether wrong.

And if there were elements of Celtic twilight and mysticism in the leadership, there were none in Connolly, who knew exactly where he was aiming to go. He wanted a Workers' Republic, and he had a tough body of Marxist theory on which to base it. Whether capitalist England, once disengaged from her "difficulty", would have tolerated a Marxist state on her doorstep is another matter. Perhaps even Connolly did not look so far ahead as that.

But the immediate prospect was less of a gamble than any previous Irish insurrection had been. There were two essentials for success: that arms should be forthcoming from Germany and from supporters in America, and that the two Nationalist forces, his own Citizen Army and the Irish Volunteers under Eoin MacNeill, should act as one. MacNeill was an easy-going professor of Celtic languages, but he had among his lieutenants resolute men like Patrick Pearse and Tom Clarke, who were prepared to supersede him when the moment came.

Meanwhile, the conspirators took their arms where they could find them, however modest the source. Margaret Skinnider, a young Irish schoolmistress living in Glasgow, brought over a set of detonators at Christmas 1915, and delivered them to Madame Markievicz at Surrey House. Constance tried them out somewhere near her mountain cottage, and succeeded in blowing up a wall. Miss Skinnider remembers meeting Connolly, short and thick-set, quiet and tense, "the answer to those who said the Rising was the work of dreamers and idealists". News came, while she was in Dublin, that a shipload of arms would arrive in Ireland on or near Easter Sunday, and her hosts promised to let her know when she would be needed again. She went home to practise rifle-shooting, determined to make herself a soldier as fully operational as was Madame.

5

As all the world knows, the Rising of Easter 1916 was doomed, militarily, before it began. The arms ship was captured, and the plans betrayed to the British Government. Eoin MacNeill countermanded the mobilisation order to the Irish Volunteers, with the result that many of them did not take up arms. The force available to seize and hold strategic points in Dublin, some 1,500 men, was about half what had been originally planned. Nevertheless, Pearse, Connolly and the other leaders decided to go ahead, even though it was tantamount to signing their own death-warrants. The Tricolour flag was hoisted at the General Post Office, and the Republic proclaimed.

Constance's part in the operation can be followed through Margaret Skinnider's account and through her own. At no time was it any part of Connolly's plan that the women of Cumann na mBan or of the Citizen Army should do any actual fighting. They were to be the cooks, the medical auxiliaries, the despatch riders. These last carried revolvers, but with strict instructions only to use them in self-defence— as Margaret Skinnider found to her chagrin when on Easter Monday she was detailed as despatch rider for the Stephens Green command.

Only two women held commissions in the Citizen Army, Constance, with the rank of staff lieutenant, and her close friend Dr. Kathleen Lynn, who was appointed medical officer with the rank of captain. Only Constance wore uniform, and her doing so was made another reproach, "a society woman parading Dublin in fancy-dress". In fact her dark green jacket was a cast-off of her friend and commander Michael Mallin's, he being a slight little man. The slouch hat with its plume of cock's feather's was her own invention, and there is certainly something at once histrionic and a trifle pathetic about that—but after all, Constance was a pioneer among modern Amazons, with no precedent to guide her. The hat must have made her an easy target, and it does not say much for British military marksmanship that she came through unscathed.

This was her moment of ecstasy, the climax of her years as an agitator. "The hour so anxiously awaited, so eagerly expected, had come at last. Our hearts' desires were granted to us, and we counted ourselves lucky." The smallness of their numbers did not disturb her in the least. Before they moved off on the Monday morning to their respective posts, she had a last talk with Tom Clarke outside Dr. Lynn's surgery. "It seems queer, looking back on it," she says, "how no one spoke of death or fear or defeat."

The plan would seem to have been that she and Dr. Lynn should tour the various positions in a staff car with medical and other supplies, but when they reached Stephens Green, Michael Mallin, who was in command there, told her that he must keep her as a sniper, because he was so desperately short of men. Thus the second part of her "heart's desire" came true. He put her in charge of the work of barricading gates and digging trenches in the Green, and two hours later promoted her to be his second-in-command. Mallin was an ex-soldier of the British Army, one of the few leaders who had had actual fighting experience, and Constance was throughout under his orders; to blame her, as some have solemnly done, for the "fiasco" of Stephens Green is thus absurd. In any case it was a "fiasco" only in the sense that with so few troops, the high buildings round it could not be held, as had been the original intention.

The little band commandeered the imposing grey stone building of the College of Surgeons as their headquarters; Constance rang the bell, and receiving no answer, blew in the lock with her revolver. Margaret Skinnider was given her first despatch for the General Post Office, and bicycled off, arriving in time to hear Pearse proclaim the Republic and to see the green, white and orange flag run up.

In the night, the British mounted a machine-gun on the roof of the Shelbourne Hotel, one of the buildings the insurgents were to have held, and the positions on the Green became untenable. They retired into the College of Surgeons and proceeded to turn it into a fortress, cutting holes in the attic roof for the snipers to fire through. Constance gleefully discovered a store of rifles and ammunition, the property of the College of Surgeons training corps, "which would no doubt have been used against us had we not reached the building first".

Fighting thereafter consisted mainly of roof-sniping, with an occasional sortie, and the reluctant Mallin was persuaded by Constance to allow Margaret Skinnider to take her turn at one of the loopholes. The main purpose of the sorties was to commandeer food; bakers' shops had shut, and bread carts disappeared from the streets, and the defenders were extremely hungry. On the Wednesday evening, Margaret Skinnider was sent out with four men to fire some houses in Harcourt Street, was hit by a sniper, and was carried back seriously wounded. "Madame" went out and avenged her. Miss Skinnider vouches for Constance's having killed three of the enemy during the fighting; Constance herself claimed more.

Miss Skinnider remembers the last days in the College as happy ones, in spite of her pain. Morale was tremendously high, and each evening when the shooting died down the men and girls, and a handful of Constance's Fianna boys, would gather in the large lecture-room to sing patriotic songs. One of them had words by Constance: *Armed for the battle Kneel we before thee* . . . Everyone who came in assured them that things were going well, and they believed that by this time the Volunteers outside Dublin must also have risen.

When, on the Sunday morning, a girl despatch rider arrived from the Post Office with the news that a general surrender had been decided on, it came as a thunderbolt. "We could hold out for days here," Constance cried, "let's die at our posts!" Mallin replied that they must obey the orders of their superiors, and Margaret Skinnider was carried across the Green into St. Vincent's Hospital, so that she should not fall wounded into enemy hands.

In the afternoon, they surrendered in good order. The British officer who came to arrest them offered Constance a seat in his car, but she preferred to march with Mallin at the head of the column.

The leaders were sent to Kilmainham Gaol, of evil memory in the long history of Irish rebellion, and there court martialled and shot with dreadful secrecy and speed. The first three, Pearse, Clarke and MacDonough, were shot on the Wednesday after the surrender, and from her cell she heard the shots. She herself was tried on the Saturday, pleaded Guilty, and stated: "I went out to fight for Ireland's freedom, and it doesn't matter what happens to me. I did what I thought was right and I stand by it." She received her death sentence radiantly, and she was not to know that it would be commuted to penal servitude for life, "solely and only," as the official documents states, "on account of her sex."

On the Monday, Mallin died, and with him two young captains who had learnt their soldiering in the Fianna. And at the end of the week Connolly, seriously wounded, was carried out on a stretcher to face the firing-squad.

1. Maud Gonne in old age, from a photograph by Horvath.

2. Maud Gonne in youth.

3. Maud Gonne leading her procession of militant women on O'Connell Bridge.

4. Constance Markievicz as a captain in the Irish Citizen Army.

5. Constance and Eva Gore-Booth in the woods at Lissadell, by Sarah Purser: one of the two pictures which put her on the road to success.

6. Sarah Purser: three pencil drawings by J. B. Yeats

7. Stained glass windows in Loughrea Cathedral: St. Brigid by Evie Hone,
Our Lady Queen of Heaven by Michael Healy.

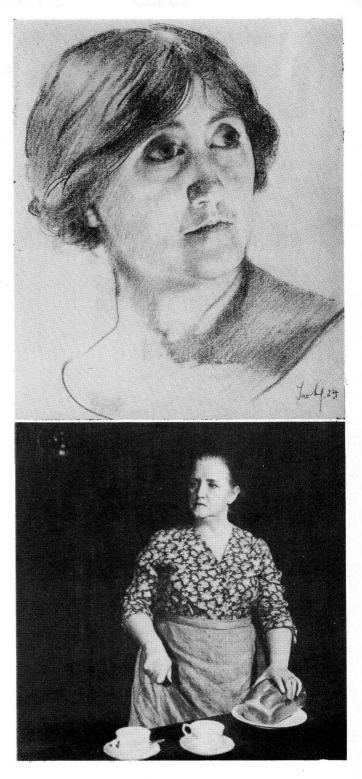

8. Sara Allgood, by Patrick Tuohy (*above*). Sara Allgood as Juno (*below*).

9.   Maire O'Neill as Pegeen Mike *(above)*. Maire O'Neill in the British Lion film *Saints and Sinners (below)*.

By this time, news had come through of Constance's reprieve, and she had been moved to Mountjoy Prison, where
her sister and Esther Roper came to visit her. They had
been told they must not speak of Connolly's execution, but
"Have they shot him?" was her first question, and their
stricken faces gave her the answer. For the first and last time
in all the many prison visits they were to pay her, she broke
down and wept. "You needn't tell me, I know. Why didn't
they let me die with my friends?" Then her courage came
back to her, she drew herself up and ended: "Well, Ireland
was free for a week."

The rest of the interview was practical: what was to be
done for comrades and dependents, and particularly for
Mallin's widow, penniless and expecting a child.

The two women went out to salvage what they could from
Surrey House, and found it ripped to pieces by the military,
its beautiful furniture and pictures destroyed. Constance was
never to have a home of her own again. And Constance
herself went back to her cell, to face the utter bleakness of
a life sentence. The time of high adventure was over; the
time for payment had begun.

6

If she had been, as her enemies alleged (and still do), a
neurotic, an exhibitionist, a mere sensation-seeker, this was
the time that would have found her out. Hitherto, a mounting excitement had swept her along, she had enjoyed the
chance to show physical courage and dash. There had
certainly been an element of self-dramatisation in her
career, and after all, why not? It is often an essential part of
character, particularly Irish character. It sweetens the

D

revolutionary's arid lot, and provided it is combined with a
sincere devotion to the cause in hand, I fail to see why it
should be considered so reprehensible. If Constance Markievicz and Maud Gonne inspired others, it was because first
of all they had the capacity to inspire themselves.

But if the splendid gesture is without solid backing,
removal of the excitement and the audience will soon betray
the fact. They could hardly have been removed with more
brutal completeness than in Constance's case, yet with each
dreary month of imprisonment she grew in stature. Her
letters to Eva, cherished and published after both sisters
were dead, are witness to that.

Mountjoy, an Irish prison, had been endurable. There
were seagulls, and soft Irish voices, and "a most attractive
convict-baby with a squint", and wardresses who would slip
out illicit letters, and little boys singing patriotic songs outside the walls. But in June she was brought over to England
and sent to the women's prison at Aylesbury, where the walls
were damp and the food uneatable; where she was just a
number, and required to turn her face to the wall if she met
anyone in the corridors. Exercise was an hour in the court-
yard each day and then floor-scrubbing; there was no one to
exchange ideas with; and on the intellectual level she faced
what was in effect solitary confinement—for life.

Her treatment, as Eva and Esther continually represented
to the Home Secretary, was far harder than that of any other
Irish "felon". The men had all been sent to Lewes Gaol,
where by a special resolution of the House of Commons they
were allowed a certain amount of association each day; where
they laid their plans for the future, and Eamonn de Valera,
the only surviving senior commander, acquired the ascen-
dancy which marked him out as the new leader. And
although the five other women interned for their part in the
Rising eventually arrived at Aylesbury, Constance as a
"lifer" was not allowed to speak to them. She had only
thieves and murderesses for company.

It goes without saying that she relished the thieves, who for their part pronounced her a good sport, and felt deeply sorry for the murderesses, mostly pathetic girls who had smothered their illegitimate babies. But they could not satisfy her hunger for news, for talk, for political discussion and plans. Nor was she supposed to put any political matter into the monthly letter to her sister, on one miserable sheet of paper, which was all she was permitted to write.

And still her quality shines out of these heavily censored documents. Her first concern is to reassure Eva: "My darling, I repeat, *don't* worry about me. I am quite cheerful and content, and I would have felt very small and useless if I had been ignored." And again, "It is in nobody's power to make me unhappy. I am not afraid, either of the future or of myself. You know well how little comforts and luxuries ever meant to me. So at the worst I'm only bored." Yet she believed that the life-sentence meant what it said: "don't count on my getting out for ever so long, unless a real fuss is made (home and America). I don't see why they should let me go."

She who had had so little time for feminine prettinesses pined now for beauty, scribbled verses, embroidered with threads drawn out from the cleaning rags she was given, and when at long last Eva got permission to supply her with drawing materials, took up her sketching again. She treasured every scrap of beauty and freedom that she could see.

"The greedy starlings are making such a row on my window-ledge, fighting most rudely over the remains of my dinner. This morning a wedge-shaped flight of wild geese flew over us as we were exercising, making their weird cackling cry, and they brought me home at once." "The one thing I am learning here is to watch everything closely, whether it is trees or black beetles, birds or women." It was a time of stocktaking and self-knowledge, after the din of battle. "All my life, in a funny way, seems to have led up to the last year, and it's all been such a hurry-scurry of a life. Now I feel that I have done what I was born to do." The visits of a sympathetic Roman Catholic chaplain helped to deepen the impression made on her by the shining faith of her comrades in Easter Week.

Another visitor was the Dowager Duchess of St. Albans, who came in an official capacity, and having known Miss Gore-Booth since her childhood, found the meeting awkward. "Do you say your prayers, my dear?" she enquired. "Well, you know," said Constance in telling the tale to Esther and Eva afterwards, "I really felt a bit insulted, but I thought I'd get my own back without showing my feelings, so I opened my eyes wide and replied: 'Of course, why, don't you?' "

Where she could, she laughed. She has been called humourless, but she could often be amusing when her political passions were not involved. "I am glad that I am President of so many things, I should always advise societies to choose their presidents from among jail-birds, as presidents are such a bore and so in the way on committees. . . ." This from one of her last letters, and marking the apotheosis that was taking place in Ireland.

The visits of Eva and Esther, wearing anything pretty they could borrow from their friends ("Always visit criminals in your best clothes," she had commanded, "blue and grey for choice if it's me!"), were her lifeline. They brought her flowers, which she somehow kept alive from one month to the next, and news of Ireland, and the news was increasingly heartening.

For the brutal stupidity of General Maxwell's firing-squads had done more than all Pearse's eloquence and Connolly's planning; opinion in Ireland seemed to change almost overnight. The deaths had reminded Irishmen, for the first time in their generation, that the cause was still there and worth dying for. Yeats published his great Easter poems, A. E. gave Constance a special accolade: "Here's to you,

Constance, in your cell!" Even English public opinion wavered. Many who had talked about a stab in the back now began to concede that the Rising had been a genuine if misguided patriotic manifestation, and that the harsh means used to suppress it had been, to say the least, unwise.

At Christmas the internees, who included all the other women, were freed, and in June of 1917 the full-dress prisoners were released. Eva was told that she might go to Aylesbury and bring her sister away. It was an astonishing homecoming. Constance had left Ireland a sinister virago; she returned a national heroine. All Dublin turned out to welcome her, and she was obliged to stand in Dr. Kathleen Lynn's car, so that she could be seen by the crowds. At Liberty Hall, still roofless from the fighting, there was an official reception committee, and behind it a group of women in mourning, the widows of her executed comrades.

Never before had an Irishwoman received such popular acclaim, not even Maud Gonne. It meant that Constance was now a power in her own right, a figure to be reckoned with in the national life. Next time that national independence was asserted, it would not be possible to keep her down.

7

Exalted but worn out, she had first to rebuild her strength under the devoted Dr. Lynn's nursing, and to put her spiritual affairs in order. She had been taking Catholic instruction in Aylesbury, and she was received into the Church that October. Like Maud Gonne, she was an unorthodox Catholic, very prone to argue with her spiritual directors, and she remained sufficiently Connolly's pupil to follow Lenin's progress closely, and to take a much warmer interest in the first real Workers' Republic than they can have considered seemly. But by and large her religion was a comfort to her, and she never appears to have reached the point where it and her Socialism clashed.

That autumn, de Valera called together the various independence movements and welded them into one under the general title of Sinn Fein, and she was elected to the executive of the reorganised body. It soon had a fight against conscription on its hands. The war with Germany was going badly and England's need for more troops was desperate; even so, it was a curious madness on the part of Lloyd George to imagine he could get them from a country which had shown itself so openly disaffected.

There was intense feeling against conscription, and on the part of many who had previously stood aloof from rebellion. But of course the authorities knew that Sinn Fein was the fountain of the resistance, and in May of 1918 more than a hundred of its leaders were arrested and interned without trial on the pretext of an imaginary "German plot". Constance, with Maud Gonne and Mrs. Tom Clarke, found herself in Holloway, her second and last taste of an English gaol.

The physical conditions of this imprisonment, and Maud Gonne's sufferings under them, have already been described. Constance, on the other hand, was cock-a-hoop. "Myself," she writes to Eva, "I think it is about the best thing that could have happened for Ireland, as there was so little to be done there, only propaganda, and our arrests carry so much further than speeches. Sending you to gaol is like pulling out all the loud stops in all the speeches you ever made or words you ever wrote." She missed, as they all did, the comfort of visitors, but the authorities' insistence on an undertaking "not to talk politics" was a tyranny to be resisted at all costs. "A little patience, and won't we talk! I feel quite capable of talking not only the hind but all four legs off that belted ass, the British Empire."

Humanly, it was a curious situation—these three Irish-women, alike in their devotion to the cause but tempera-mentally so different, cooped up together in the claustro-phobic atmosphere of the prison wing set apart for them. Constance had long admired Maud Gonne, had to some extent been inspired by her, and this admiration continued, but it was overlaid by a good thick layer of mutual irritants now that they were so painfully close.

Maud and Kathleen Clarke were tortured by anxiety about their children; to Constance, who had cheerfully relinquished her daughter to others' care, this maternal solicitude carried overtones of reproach. They on their side were now and then provoked by her airs of professional revolutionary and old lag. She and Maud, Mrs. Clarke remembers, would bicker over small social snobberies, of no real account to either of them. Towards Mrs. Clarke herself, Constance's manner was extravagantly protective—"I can't imagine why they arrested you, such a frail, inoffensive little thing as you are." "At last I rounded on her," Mrs. Clarke recalls, "and said, 'Little and inoffensive I may be, but my charge-sheet is the same as yours,' and after that she shut up." As always, Constance meant well, and her tactlessness must have been thrown into glaring relief by the proximity of Maud Gonne, all femininity and charm.

Fundamentally, they respected each other, and of course presented a united front to the common enemy, refusing any concessions to one that were not made to all. Then in December came Maud Gonne's transfer to a sanatorium on health grounds, followed in February by that of Mrs. Clarke (whose health in fact gave much greater cause for concern), and Constance was left alone. She missed them badly, and even looked back on Aylesbury with regret. "At Aylesbury we had a certain community of hatred that gave one mutual interests, and the mutual sport of combining to pinch onions, dripping or rags. Doesn't it sound funny and mad?—but it kept one going."

But as a period of preparation and reflection, this intern-ment was valuable to her. She was allowed books, and she read voraciously, particularly political economy, to equip herself for a position in the independent Irish Government which must surely lie just round the corner. She knew the very position she wanted, the Ministry for Labour. There, she would be best placed to carry on Connolly's crusade, and see to it that national freedom meant first and foremost a better life for the working people.

In the General Election of 1918, women for the first time could stand as candidates for the British Parliament. Con-stance's name was put forward for the St. Patrick's Division of Dublin, and she was elected—one of seventy-three Sinn Fein candidates to be returned, and thirty-six of them in prison. It was a triumph beyond even the party's hopes, and for Constance it also meant a tiny niche in the history of the Mother of Parliaments. She received in Holloway a printed letter, signed by Lloyd George, inviting her to take her seat.

There would have been no question of her doing so, even had she been free, as Sinn Fein had decided to boycott the House of Commons and form its own Republican Parlia-ment, Dail Eireann. The first meeting of this body—without, of course, the imprisoned deputies—took place next month. Constance's connexion with the Palace of Westminster was confined to her name on a cloakroom peg, and some time later, when staying with Esther Roper, she went incognito and had a look at it. Lady Astor, returned for the Sutton division of Plymouth at a by-election that summer, was the first woman Member actually to take her seat.

De Valera made his dramatic escape from Lincoln Gaol, and in March, as a result of public protests, all the Irish internees were released. Constance came home to a welcome as rapturous as the last, took her seat in the second Dail Eireann, under the presidency of Mr. de Valera, and claimed her reward.

She that but little patience knew. . . . Once again Yeats, in a high-sounding poem, has conferred the wrong sort of immortality. It was Maud Gonne's imprisonment, not Constance's, that moved him, and he admitted in a letter that he was writing a poem on Constance to avoid writing one on Maud. Constance was to know five imprisonments in all, and to bear them with a quite exemplary patience, regarding them as a necessary and even valuable part of a revolutionary's life.

And neither woman really deserved the jibe about the mind that had become a bitter, abstract thing. Both of them, at this juncture particularly, were filled with generous and very concrete plans for the betterment of their less fortunate countrymen. Both of them cared about conditions in the Dublin slums and the country cabins, cared with a passion that makes his preoccupation with "ceremony" look tinsel. Would it not have done more honour to a great poet, to have seen the intrinsic nobility that lay behind the occasional surface follies of these lives? Instead, he has left us his regret that the one would not allow herself to be diminished into a literary salon ornament, and the other confine herself to hunting, dancing and gracious living amid the broad acres of Lissadell.

8

Constance claimed her reward, and was duly appointed Minister for Labour in Mr. de Valera's first Cabinet. She was wild with excitement and delight. "I took a gun to their heads," she told Kathleen Clarke, "I said I'd go over to Labour if they didn't." It was not a very dangerous threat, as the Irish Labour Party (Connolly's foundation) had agreed not to oppose Sinn Fein at the election; and as she explained to Eva: "I belong to both organisations, for my conception of a free Ireland is economic as well as political; some agree with me, some don't, but it's not a sore point. Easter Week comrades don't fall out; they laugh and chaff and disagree. It annoys the enemy considerably."

But before she could do more than brief her staff, "the enemy" paid her the compliment of again arresting her, this time on a charge of making a seditious speech at Mallow, and she served four months in Cork Gaol, "the most comfortable jail I've been in yet". The people of Cork sent her in fruit and flowers, and three cooked meals a day.

And maddening though it was to have the cup of power snatched from her lips, she endured it with her usual philosophy. "My getting locked up has done more to bring women out into the open than anything else," she wrote to Eva. "The shyest are ready to do my work when I'm not there." This diffidence and lack of political self-confidence on the part of her countrywomen never ceased to concern her, for as she pointed out, they could and did behave like heroines in suffering or under fire. "Outside the towns, they want their initiative faculties developing," she wrote later. "There has been less physical restraint on the actions of women in Ireland than in any other country, but mentally the restrictions seem to me very oppressive."

She worked on plans for realising her part of Connolly's aims. "Of course there are endless possibilities in the economic situation in Ireland. . . . Since the war all kinds of new regulations against Ireland's trade and commerce have been started. In the case of fixed prices, Ireland always gets less for the same or even superior goods. The old Sinn Fein organisation started on this, but you can do so little with an enemy in occupation of your country. Directly we get the Republic into working order we shall do a lot."

She came out of gaol in October 1919, to find that the Dail, which had been functioning against increasing opposition

from the British Government, had finally been suppressed
and gone underground. The full body could no longer meet,
but the Cabinet met weekly, always in a different house, and
the various Ministries were carried on from basements and
hiding-places, also frequently changed. The entire "ministry"
probably consisted of a desk for the chief, and another for a
couple of secretaries.

The astonishing story of this "Dail on the run", which
from its hide-outs gradually transferred the British Government's authority to itself, has never been fully told. It
appealed to the Irish people for a loan, and they subscribed
a quarter of a million pounds. It levied rates, settled land
disputes with a fairness which even the Unionists recognised,
drew up schemes for the utilisation of water-power and
the furthering of trade. And of all the departments, none
was more successful than Constance's, the Ministry for
Labour.

Industrial disputes were referred to it by both sides, and
at one time it was handling thirty-five a month and settling
65 per cent. of them. In addition, it issued orders that men
of the Royal Irish Constabulary who resigned for patriotic
reasons should be offered employment or else assisted from a
special fund, and that members should be approached
through their relatives and urged to resign. And one of its
biggest achievements was to co-operate in, and later take
charge of, an effective boycott of Ulster manufactures.

Constance's detractors have been much too ready to give
credit for these successes to her deputy, Joseph McGrath,
and certainly Mr. McGrath has proved his abilities in a
subsequent career which has made him one of the wealthiest
men in Ireland. But the idealism, the vision, the directing
brain were hers.

She never missed the weekly meeting of the Cabinet, nor
of her Fianna, adopting the various disguises which have
become part of Dublin legend (her favourite was a crone in
an old black bonnet bobbing with cherries), and she flew

about Dublin on a battered bicycle; "every house is open to me, and everyone ready to help". Michael Collins was co-ordinating what had begun as sporadic resistance move-ments into a full-scale guerrilla war against the British army of occupation, and amid her other duties she found time to be a fiery and effective recruiting officer. "You don't know what a joke it is," she told Eva, "sometimes to speak at meetings and get through with it in spite of their guns and tanks and soldiers and police." This year of liberty was undoubtedly the happiest and most constructive of her life.

The inevitable re-arrest came on September 26th, 1920. She was kept in Mountjoy for two months without trial, then faced a court martial on a charge of conspiracy (this related to the Fianna, which, as she pointed out, had never been secret), and of organising the killing of soldiers. "Such an ordeal as it was!" she wrote to Kathleen Clarke. "You feel so bewildered getting into a crowd like that after two months' solitude . . . a court martial like that would be a very good scene in a melodrama, most pathetic! One lone woman surrounded by bayonets and tin hats, facing innumerable accusing and judging men, last comic stroke, the Englishman in wig and gown, it must have looked awfully funny." The sentence this time was two years' hard labour.

She settled down in Mountjoy to more self-education ("Jail is the only place where one gets time to read"), tried—unsuccessfully—to teach herself Irish, and made a rock-garden. She looked back on her Labour achievement with quiet pride. "Well—I got it under way so that it goes on just as well without me. That wasn't too bad for an untried fool, was it?" Conditions in the prison were hard, but she urged Eva not to worry. "The English ideal of modern civilisation always galled me. Endless relays of exquisite food and the eternal changing of costume bored me always to tears." And by being in prison for a third winter, she did at least escape the worst horrors of the Black and Tan war.

The Truce of July 1921, which was the preliminary to the

Treaty negotiations, freed her, together with all other imprisoned or interned members of Dail Eireann. The Dail met in August and re-elected de Valera as its president, and he re-appointed Constance to the Ministry for Labour.

"It's so heavenly to be out again and to be able to shut and open doors," she wrote to Eva. "It is almost worth while being locked up, for the great joy release brings. Life is so wonderful. One just wanders round and enjoys it. The children and the trees and cows and all common things are so heavenly after nothing but walls and uniformed people. It is too funny, suddenly to be a Government and supposed to be respectable! One has to laugh."

That she used her new "respectability" with sense and moderation is shown by this letter to Edward M. Stephens, a well-known Dublin solicitor, who although a Nationalist was far from being a Republican and was known for his opposition to violence:

> Dail Eireann, Dept. of Labour,
> Mansion House, 29th Nov. 1921.

Dear Mr. Stephens,

I am writing to ask you if you would consent to act occasionally for me as Arbitrator in Labour disputes. I believe that your name would be one that would inspire confidence to both sides. I am very anxious to have a few such names as yours on our panels, that I can call on in important and delicate cases, men too with either general knowledge of business or with a technical knowledge of any certain business.

> Mise, do Chara,*
> Constance de Markievicz.
> Minister for Labour.

The Treaty delegation headed by Griffith and Collins had been in London since October, and although it was known that Lloyd George was deploying every wile and threat against them, still nobody doubted that they would return

---

* I am, your friend.

with a full-dress Irish Republic in their pockets. Instead, they
came home in December with the document which provided
for a "Free State" in southern Ireland, within the Common-
wealth. The Utopia on which Constance and the other dyed-
in-the-wool Republicans had placed such sanguine hopes
was gone with the wind.

9

It is possible for the English visitor today to move about
Ireland and feel that seven hundred years of oppression are
forgotten; but he cannot mistake the traumatic effects of the
Treaty split and the resultant Civil War. People are still not
on speaking terms; scars were inflicted which will not be
forgotten till all who bear them are in the grave.

One result of this appalling national experience is a
continued search for scapegoats. *Cherchez la femme* is a
favourite expedient. The women fomented bitterness, one is
told, and the women deputies in particular; "they egged
Dev on". Constance, being the best known, is apt to top the
black list.

Certainly they were all six of them vehement against the
Treaty, but if Mr. de Valera had a female *éminence grise*, it was
Mary MacSwiney, and not Constance, for whom it is doubtful if he felt any great sympathy. She was rather too much of
a Socialist for his taste, while he (although she was loyal to
him as the Republican leader) was rather too much of a
visionary and mystic for hers. But those who know Mr. de
Valera best consider it unlikely that he was ever swayed, by
man or woman, in any direction which he had not already
determined to take.

In her speech in the Treaty debate, Constance invoked

Connolly's memory. They had been told, she said, that they did not know what they meant by a Republic. "Now I know what I mean—a State run by the Irish people for the people. That means a Government that looks after the rights of people before the rights of property, and I don't wish under the Saorstat to anticipate that the directors of property and the capitalists' interests are to be the head of it. My idea is the Workers' Republic for which Connolly died, and a real Treaty between a free Ireland and a free England. . . . That is the thing that I can grasp in my nature. I have seen the stars and I am not going to follow a flickering will-o'-the-wisp."

In an article in the Glasgow-printed revolutionary paper *Eire* at a later date, she set out her objections to the Treaty less emotionally and more specifically. They were: that the British Government still held the principal ports and had the right to establish and garrison Air Stations; that the Irish Government had no power to amend the Constitution, which included the oath of allegiance to the King; that no money could be appropriated without the consent of the King's Representative; that no Bill could become law without the King's assent; that judges were appointed by the King's Representative. Under these conditions, she considered, "the wearing by the Government of the badge and green uniform of the I.R.A., the flying of the Tricolor flag under which we fought, is a trickery".

Well, it is tempting to apply hindsight, and tell Constance across the years that this insistence on the letter of what was fought for will open the way to a worse bloodshed; tempting to sympathise with Michael Collins in his passionate plea that what he has brought back from London is the basis of freedom, and the rest will follow in due course; tempting to applaud Kevin O'Higgins, the ablest person on the Cosgrave side, when a few years later he seriously proposes that as a way to end Partition King George shall come to Dublin and be crowned King of Ireland.

But that would be to ignore the march of history, the climate of opinion, the enormous emotional pressure that had been building up ever since the Rising. That the Oath of Allegiance was an empty formula to be muttered and forgotten—that the British would never have risked using Irish ports in the face of Irish opposition—that the King's Representative could be by-passed on every important issue —that the King, wherever he was crowned, would have no more real authority in Ireland than he had in Canada—none of that signifies.

No nation lives by bread alone, and the Irish, who have had so little bread in their unhappy history, live more than most of us by the Word, the Symbol, the Myth. Thousands of them had lived and died for the Republic, for Kathleen ni Houlihan, for the righting of the wrong done by Dervorgilla's treachery, for a cause that went back beyond memory and sometimes beyond reason. They could not alter now. They could not accept an amicable compromise, and leave time to dissolve the inconsistencies out, without murdering something in themselves.

So instead (the cynic may say) they murdered each other. What we who come afterwards have to remember is that these people were caught in a tragic dilemma, that neither side had a monopoly of integrity and high conviction, and that it is for us not to judge, but to attempt to understand.

On January 7th, 1922, the Dail accepted the Treaty by a mere seven votes. De Valera resigned the presidency and Arthur Griffith reigned in his stead; McGrath, Constance's deputy at the Ministry for Labour, reigned in hers. Her parliamentary career was almost over. But her share in the Dail debates of March show that in spite of her fierce preoccupation with the Treaty, she still cared about people; she might be "bitter" but she was not "abstract". Particularly she cared about women. Supporting a proposal to give land to I.R.A. members with farming experience, she urged "that some land be given to women, who are just as capable of running farms as men are, I have seen it demonstrated myself".

And she supported her friend Mrs. O'Callaghan's motion to extend the franchise to the younger women—speaking with some difficulty, since a deputy named O'Keefe had tried to close the debate, exclaiming that "an O'Keefe will never yield to a Gore-Booth". She pointed out that though she herself had the vote, it was denied to women under thirty, "who proved their valour during the years of the Terror in a way that we, the older women, never got a chance to do". Cathal Brugha, that grim warrior, was an unexpected ally. He reminded the Dail of the part played by women in the Easter Rising. "Most of you know that that enterprise was not received too popularly by the Irish public during Easter week or immediately after. But it was the women, when they organised the public Masses and the public meetings as far as they could, who kept the spirit alive, who kept the flame alive and the flag flying."

But Arthur Griffith was no more appreciative of the women's share in the liberation movement than de Valera and Parnell had been before him. To pass the motion might, he said, "torpedo the Treaty", and it was lost by nine votes.

10

At this disheartening juncture, the assignment of an American lecture tour which came Constance's way was very welcome. De Valera when in the U.S.A. had been notably successful in attracting well-to-do, second-generation Irish-American support for the liberation movement, and it was now needful to explain to these bewildered adherents what had gone wrong, and to ensure that their support should continue to the Republican opposition, and not to the Provisional Government which was shortly to develop into that of the Irish Free State.

A delegation of speakers was sent out under the leadership of Austin Stack, who had been Minister for Home Affairs. The two women chosen for it were Constance, and Kathleen Barry, a sister of Kevin Barry, the young medical student, hanged during the Black and Tan war, whose name had already passed into folksong and legend.

Constance and Miss Barry sailed on the *Aquitania* at the end of March, Miss Barry with private instructions from de Valera to "keep Madame on the rails"; she was to be every inch the Countess. The American press gave them a generous accolade, the title of "Joan of Arc of Ireland", which had already been accorded to Maud Gonne, passing to Constance. "The best known and most romantic character in the Irish Republican movement," the papers found, and the *New York Tribune* for April 8th described her as "a pale fragile woman, with light fluffy hair and wide blue eyes— obviously one of the soft, sweet, unyielding sort. . . . Countess Markievicz is a figure to be reckoned with in Ireland, not alone because of the white heat of her revolutionary zeal, but because of something about her that kindles the imagination of the people. She is such a personality as the Irish have always had for their leaders—quixotic and shrewd, mystical and wayward, a woman who lived a romantic eventful life of exile before she came back to take part in her country's affairs." (This last phrase would seem to give her art-student days in London and Paris rather more importance than they deserve.)

She certainly made a good news story, with plenty of quotes. "The Gandhi programme of boycott was copied from us. I have not a stitch on me of anything that was made in England. The blouse I wear was made in the White Cross shops established with American money. The skirt I wear was made in the co-operative tailoring shop in Abbey Street in Dublin."

She carried the fiery cross all through the Middle West. "Ireland will never accept the Treaty, and she is prepared to shed more blood rather than have it thrust upon her." The *Butte Miner* for April 28th found her "aristocratic in mien, in dress and in every gesture and tone", and admired her black dress trimmed with red braid and "fetching many-coloured hat" (evidently Mr. de Valera's instructions on dress and deportment were being observed). She for her part, when taken down a copper-mine, insisted on penetrating beyond the main passages, and asked awkward questions about the heat and dust and the heavy death-rate from tuberculosis.

The *Anaconda Standard* for April 29th reported her "brilliant" description of Easter Week. "For one week we hunted the English around Dublin," she told her audience, "and we knew how it felt to be men; how it felt to look down the barrel of a gun at an Englishman's heart."

The tour was to have lasted four months, but when they reached San Francisco they were summoned home to take part in the "Pact" election of June 24th, when for the first and only time Constance lost her seat. This had small practical significance, as the Republican deputies had decided to boycott the Dail as formerly they had boycotted Westminster. But it did mean that when during the Civil War de Valera formed his opposition shadow cabinet, a body with a strong aura of Celtic Twilight about it which met from time to time "on the run", Constance was not among the members.

Tension had been mounting steadily; soon after the departure of the delegation for America, Republican troops under Rory O'Connor, who had been one of the first boy recruits to Constance's Fianna, had occupied the Four Courts in Dublin and were openly defying the government of Griffith and Collins. On June 28th, Collins retaliated by

ordering the shelling of the building. Constance, needless to
say, did not hesitate. This was the beginning of the Civil War
she had prophesied to her American audiences, and once
more she had a gun in her hands.

I I

This time she had no command, but served, first under
Oscar Traynor and then under Cathal Brugha, at the Ham-
mam Hotel in O'Connell Street, which had been seized by
the insurgents as their G.H.Q. She is remembered as
sniping from the windows of various houses up and down the
street; once again, the only woman armed, though girls of
Cumann na mBan were cooking, despatch-riding, carrying
arms and doing First Aid work as they had done in 1916.
And once again, she was in one of the last buildings to hold
out, and protested bitterly when told of the imminent
surrender. Kathleen Barry remembers the little scene:
Brugha saying "Madame, I order you as a soldier to hand
over your rifle," and Constance doing it in a split second and
marching down the room to the back door.

The Government, doubtless having no wish to turn a
national heroine into a martyr, allowed her to escape and
join the other Republican leaders "on the run". And for the
next year, most of her time was spent out of the country,
either in England, speaking at anti-Treaty meetings which
were always liable to be raided by the police, or in Scotland,
where she helped to produce the Republican paper *Eire*,
published from Glasgow. Her movements in Ireland during
this year of civil war are lost in a fog of violence, secrecy and
gloom.

The grim guerrilla war dragged on till the end of the

following April, when resistance to what was always, for Constance, "the Freak State" officially ceased and the Republicans laid down their arms, leaving thousand of prisoners in Government hands. The tide of sympathy was beginning to turn in their favour, and to the general surprise they secured forty-four seats in the election of August 1923, although many of their candidates were in hiding or in gaol. Constance regained St. Patrick's, now re-christened Dublin South—though as she would not take the Oath of Allegiance there could still be no question of her taking her seat.

That winter the men and women in the internment camps and in Mountjoy went on hunger-strike, and for day after day Constance was out in her constituency, haranguing the crowds from a lorry and urging them to sign petitions for the prisoners' release. Inevitably she was arrested, for the fifth and last time, and sent to a disused Dublin workhouse, "a vast and gloomy place, haunted by the ghosts of broken-hearted paupers", where she immediately went on hunger-strike herself.

As she told Eva afterwards, the worst part of it was making the decision, "the sort of shrinking that one has before taking a header into a cold sea. After that I did not suffer at all but just stayed in bed and dozed and tried to prepare myself to leave the world. I was perfectly happy and had no regrets." The calling-off of the hunger-strike by her superiors "woke me up with a jump, and it was like coming to life again and I wanted to live and I wanted the others to live". She was released in time for Christmas.

Home in these last years was a room in the house of her friends the Coughlins at Rathmines. Frankfort House was another of those big, "rebelly" suburban homes where the hostess might not know how many she had sheltered till breakfast-time. The Coughlin children remember "Maddy" as a cheerful, bustling guest who stood in an aunt-like relation to them, and would frequently pack them into her rattling second-hand Ford car for picnics in the mountains, or let them loose in the aisles of Woolworth's while she shopped in Grafton Street. Their affection for her was tinged with that embarrassment which children will feel in the company of an adult who is consistently conspicuous. Nobody in Dublin could fail to recognise "the Coun*tess*;" she had become a civic monument.

But I cannot see any grounds for her previous biographer's* suggestion that she was now a back number and that her political usefulness was over. Her hold on her constituents, and on the Dublin crowds, was as strong as ever, and so was her faith in the revival of the Republican fortunes. She was a national figure, and if she had lived it would not have been possible for Mr. de Valera to pass her over, nor likely that he would have wished to.

Early in 1926, he re-formed his forces into a new party, Fianna Fail, a preliminary step along the tortuous path which was to get them back into the Dail. Constance joined the party, it is said with misgivings; she was observed at an early meeting to have tears in her eyes. But that she was less intransigent now, more aware of the need for political manœuvre, is shown by her last letter to Eva:

"I wonder what you think of us all? I sometimes think that people get rather mad when they go in for politics. The latest has made me laugh since it began. Dev, I say like a wise man, has announced that he will go into the Free State Parliament if there is no oath, and this has caused an unholy row. I myself have always said that the oath made it absolutely impossible for an honourable person who was a Republican to go in, and that if it were removed, it would then be simply a question of policy with no principle involved, whether we went in or stayed out. Dev thinks the moment has come to start attacking the Oath and demanding its removal. Some unlogical persons are howling. They stand for principle and for the honour of the Republic and prefer to do nothing but shout continually 'The Republic lives!'

* *Constance Markievicz*, by Sean O'Faolain.

. . . I think the ordinary man and woman in the street will agree with us. I don't think we'll get the Oath removed, at any rate for a long time, but anyhow it is something to go for with a chance of success, and something outside Ireland might help."

Eva Gore-Booth died in June of 1926, worn out by incessant work for pacifist causes and on behalf of refugees. The shock to Constance was severe. Though the sisters were not often together, the link between them never slackened, and her every thought and hope had always been poured out in those vivid slangy letters to her "dearest old darling". She had always recognised the high quality in Eva, the courage that opposed tyranny by gentleness and not by violence, though she could not bring herself to believe that it would have answered in the Irish struggle. Esther Roper, who saw her in London later that year, thought her looking very ill, and put it down to grief; but it is probable that the cancer which was to kill her had already taken hold.

However, she denied that anything was wrong. She continued to drill her Scouts and to work for the new party; when, that winter, the coal strike brought hardship to the poor homes of her constituency, she took the little car out to the mountains, filled the back of it with turf and wood, and toiled up flights of slum stairs with fuel in a rucksack. Even this has been made the subject of sneers; "anyone would have been delighted to carry the fuel for her". But that is to mistake altogether the nature of her feeling for the poor. Even as a Daughter of the Great House, she had ousted the laundress from the tub and sat up herself with the sick groom; now, she had become a neighbour, "mere Irish", one of themselves. In the course of her political career she had sometimes had to delegate authority, but she never learned to delegate kindness.

The election of June 1927 was the last of her whirlwind political campaigns. She was out all day speaking from her little car, broke her arm in two places cranking it, got the nearest doctor to splint it with a cheerful "Glory be, it's my arm and not my jaw, I can still talk," and went on to the next meeting. She was again returned by a big majority, and shared in the attempt of de Valera and the other Fianna Fail deputies to enter the Dail without actually taking the Oath.

The collapse came next month. She seems to have believed it was appendicitis, and chose a bed in the public ward of a slum hospital, saying that what was good enough for the poor was good enough for her. A broadcast appeal was sent out to the little family she had loved and forgotten; Casimir and her stepson came over from Poland, her daughter and Esther Roper from London. Casimir was much moved, and showed Miss Roper a bundle of his old love-letters that he had found in her desk. "In all the years there never was an unkind word between us," he said.

The splendid constitution which had survived five imprisonments struggled for days against this last enemy, while outside the hospital crowds prayed, and the half-dozen patients in the ward with her would scarcely speak lest she should be disturbed. The end came on July 15th. "It's so beautiful," she said on that last day, "to have had all this love and kindness before I go."

Dublin gave her a tremendous funeral, with a lying-in-state guarded by her Fianna boys (it is estimated that a hundred thousand people filed before the coffin), and a procession through packed streets to the Republican Plot in Glasnevin, where Mr. de Valera spoke the oration. Doubtless there were those who came for the spectacle, but to the great majority she was a friend and a symbol gone. The story of the bed in the public ward had crowned her legend. She was "mere Irish" indeed.

She had her detractors, who would not be long in raising their voices against her memory. But they did not come from the Republican "hard core", in spite of her having followed de Valera into Fianna Fail. And they never came from the working class.

12

There are, of course, still people who regard the lives of both Maud Gonne and Constance Markievicz with something approaching horror. But even among their admirers, one finds a frequent and interesting cleavage of opinion. For those who were seduced by Maud's dazzling charm ("she was so lovely you'd forgive her anything") Constance is altogether too brash, aggressive and "English". And those to whom Maud seemed a self-advertising *poseuse* will glow when they turn to speak of Constance—"Ah, there was a woman with a great heart."

But the few survivors of those days who worked closely with them both are better able to appreciate that each made her special contribution. Constance, for all her tactlessness, could go into a movement and become part and parcel of it, whereas Maud, for all her charm, was fundamentally an individualist, and happiest running her own small—and sometimes not so small—show. And as for personifying Kathleen ni Houlihan, either could do that upon occasion; which seems to imply that Kathleen is a much more varied and inspiring character than the conventional representations of her would at all suggest.

Upon present-day Irishwomen, regularly reproached by their own press for the small part they play in public affairs, the careers of Gonne and Markievicz make disappointingly little impact. Many, I suspect, do not even remember quite who they were and what they did. But here is a contemporary woman writer paying tribute to "the Anglo-Irish Valkyries of our national resurgence":

In military uniform, some enacted the part of Brünnhilde with a brilliance that rivalled any stage artist. It is impossible to over-estimate the influence the dramatic genius of Irish and Anglo-Irish women has had over Irish life. One thinks of Countess Markievicz, "Speranza" (Lady Wilde), Lady Gregory and many more. We would not now have a republic in the south if it had not been for the women. When I say dramatic gifts, I do not mean insincerity. I mean the aptitude for a gesture, a word, a striking pose that led men to identify national heroines with the personification of Eire herself.*

Without the unspectacular courage of Republican women in their thousands, freedom could not have been won. Whether these two spectacular women had a decisive influence on the course of history is more questionable. But one can at least say that though the Republic would probably have come into being without them, its emotional climate would not have been quite the same.

What they were and are is beacon fires. They remind us all, but my sex particularly, that there is a greater good than the immediate good of hearth and home. Whatever one's views on Irish politics, or on woman's place in society, or on the right of poets to misrepresent character in imperishable verse, it should be possible to contemplate these two lives with the emotion aroused in the pacifist Eva Gore-Booth by the executions after the Easter Rising:

Grief for the noble dead
Of one who did not share their strife,
And mourned that any blood was shed,
Yet felt the broken glory of their state,
Their strange heroic questioning of Fate,
Ribbon with gold the rags of this our life.

* Olivia Robertson, *It's an Old Irish Custom.*

SOURCES:

Countess Markievicz: *Prison Letters*. London, Longmans, 1934. (Contains a biographical introduction by Esther Roper, and Constance's own account of her part in the Easter Rising.)

Sean O'Faolain: *Countess Markievicz or the Average Revolutionary*. London, Cape, 1934.

Eva Gore-Booth: *Poems*. London, Longmans, 1929.

Padraic Colum: *Arthur Griffith*. Dublin, Browne & Nolan, 1959.

P. O. Cathasaigh [i.e. Sean O'Casey]: *The Story of The Irish Citizen Army*. Dublin, Maunsel, 1919.

John Waldron: *Ireland, a Historical Review*. Dublin, Duffy, 1958.

Terence de Vere White: *Kevin O'Higgins*. London, Methuen, 1948.

Files of *The United Irishman* and *Eire*.

Recollections of Mrs. Tom Clarke, Mrs. Kathleen Barry Moloney, Miss Helena Molony, Miss Margaret Skinnider, Miss J. B. Clayton, "John Brennan", Mrs. Louie O'Brien, Mrs. Verschoyle.

Sarah Purser

AND THE TOWER OF GLASS

I

WITH THE exceptions of Jack Yeats and Evie Hone, the painters of the Irish Renascence are little regarded in Ireland itself, and virtually unknown outside. When a London exhibition was held of the work of Evie Hone, the English art critics treated her as though she were an isolated phenomenon, instead of being the fine flower (or, it can be claimed, one of the three or four fine flowers) of a creative upsurge which had run parallel with the literary and dramatic one, finding similar origins and inspiration in the Ireland of fifty years before.

One reason for this neglect is that the most important group of artists expressed themselves through the medium of stained-glass, which does not "travel" to exhibitions, and that their work must be sought out in widely scattered Irish and English churches. When any large body of it is brought together in a single church, as for example in the exquisite little cathedral of Loughrea in County Galway, the result comes as a revelation; one needs to go back to Chartres for a parallel.

Even less appreciated than the stained-glass painters themselves have been the two people who were the organisers and engineers of their achievement. Edward Martyn is remembered chiefly as a rich man who helped finance Yeats's and Lady Gregory's first theatrical venture, and then got cold feet. And although she is a much-relished figure of Dublin anecdote, nothing like adequate credit—as portrait painter, patroness, impresario, and creator of the most influential stained-glass workship of modern times—has been accorded to Miss Sarah Henrietta Purser.

2

She was the middle child in a family of eleven, nine boys and two girls, born to Benjamin Purser, flour miller of Dungarvan, and his wife Anne Mallet, of the noted family of iron-founders. The Pursers, originally from Tewkesbury, had come into Ireland as brewers in the 18th century and three generations of them were closely and profitably associated with Guinness. Sarah's grandfather, John Purser Junior, was a partner, her uncle and her father were both apprenticed to the great brewery; but whereas John Tertius Purser went on to become almost equal with Lord Iveagh in its administration, Benjamin, always more of an individualist and rolling stone, tried two small brewing ventures of his own before settling on the flour mills, at first with success.

Sarah was born on March 22nd, 1848, at Kingstown, where her mother happened to be on a visit; but the family home was at Dungarvan, and it was an exceptionally lively and intelligent one, for academic as well as commercial ability ran in the Purser blood. The daughters had better educational chances than most middle-class Irish girls at that date, for they were sent to a boarding school in Switzerland run by Moravians. They could not, of course, follow their brothers to Trinity (where two were ultimately to become professors), and the story that Sarah taught herself Greek in emulation of her brother Louis Claude is probably a myth.

Schooldays over, she was obliged to confine herself to the amateur painting and music that were considered suitable occupations for a young lady, and acquired considerably more than usual amateur proficiency in both. But she grew up able to pit her wits against those of clever boys, and relishing the cut and thrust of good talk, more perhaps, than any other pleasure in the world.

Then in 1873 occurred the disaster which was to have so profound an effect on Sarah's character and fortunes. The flour mills failed, put out of business, it is said, by American competition—but Benjamin's previous career suggests that one at least of the family abilities had passed him by.

No Purser ever went bankrupt, but it needed the combined efforts of the clan to save Benjamin from complete ruin. He went abroad, dying in Carolina in 1899. Sarah seems to have felt the disgrace as that of an actual bankruptcy. She settled with her mother very modestly in Dublin, letting it be known that she no longer expected any friends to call on them, and for a time lived on the charity of her brothers, while struggling to equip herself to earn her own bread.

Of her two talents, music would mean teaching, an idea she disliked; whereas portraiture could be made to pay. She learned what she could in classes at the Dublin School of Art, and presently decided that this was not professional equipment enough. Already more cosmopolitan in outlook than most of her Dublin contemporaries, she determined to take a course at Julien's in Paris, accepted a gift of £30 from her brothers, and on that sum lived and studied for the hardest six months of her life.

The famous Julien's was not in the full sense an art-school, but rather an *atelier*, providing painting-rooms, models and criticism from the proprietor (he had been a gymnast), reinforced by that of Academicians who looked in from time to time. The teaching was conventional, on the lines of Millet and of Yeats's bugbear Bastien-Lepage; the Impressionists were still "wild men", though Sarah may well have met some of them. But she had not gone there with any lofty notions of art for art's sake; she wished to be a marketable painter. In much the same spirit, and at much the same time, did the young John Sargent approach the *atelier* of Carolus-Durand.

E

Julien had established a "ladies' section" in an attic under the leads, in the teeth of considerable Mrs. Grundy opposition; and here Sarah found a cosmopolitan group of girls, French, Swiss, Greek, Scandinavian, Russian, all of them with one exception as poor and hardworking as herself. The star was Louise Breslau, a Swiss of real talent, and the rich exception was Marie Bashkirtseff, who has immortalised Julien's in her extraordinary Diaries, a febrile blend of insight and conceit.

Sarah does not figure much in the Diaries. She admired the beautiful Russian from a distance, and was pleased by the gift of an overall, which in after years she would wear for specially favoured sitters. But at thirty, she was much the oldest and most serious of the band, with no time to waste on cerebral love-affairs and agonies of soul, nor on the raging jealousy that Marie felt for superior talent.

Sarah, now and for the rest of her life, was always attracted to superior talent; it is perhaps her outstanding and most valuable quality. She made a lasting friend of Lulu Breslau, who has left an exquisite, Manet-like portrait of her in her Paris days. It shows a tense and pitifully thin young woman in a shabby black dress and bonnet, and indeed Sarah recalled that she was often actually hungry during those six months. Even in 1878, it was not very easy to live in Paris on little more than a pound a week.

She returned to Dublin a professional, took a little studio at 2 Leinster Street, and first exhibited in the Royal Hibernian Academy of 1880. Her first "lucky" commission, she told Thomas MacGreevy long afterwards, was to paint the beautiful Miss Frances L'Estrange of Sligo, "a very good portrait and everybody liked it".* Miss L'Estrange gave her an

---

* It was Miss L'Estrange's lucky portrait too, for the sight of it in the R.H.A. attracted her future husband to seek an introduction. I am indebted for this charming detail to Mr. Diarmuid Coffey, their son.

introduction to Lady Gore-Booth, and she was invited down to Lissadell "to paint Con and Eva, and that went well. Then Lady Gore's brother being at the Viceregal Lodge I was called in there, and he got me a few commissions for portraits in London. They were hung in the Royal Academy, and from that I never looked back—I went through the British aristocracy like the measles."

These early portraits, still cherished by the descendants of their sitters, tell one a great deal about Sarah Purser as an artist. The study of Miss L'Estrange has the opulence of dress and mien that delighted late Victorian taste, and fully explains Sarah's commercial success. The picture of the two small girls—Constance twelve, Eva ten—has something more, a real penetration into character. They are idyllically gathering flowers in a wood, but it is not just hindsight that perceives in Eva the future poet, in Con the future warrior.

Beside Miss L'Estrange's picture hangs one of her son, Diarmuid Coffey, painted in 1909, and it is utterly different in style; it might almost be by Sickert. And two more facts emerge: that Miss Purser was happiest painting clever people, especially clever men, and that her art was to some extent derivative, taking on the flavour of whatever superior talent was attracting her hero-worship at the moment. For all her independence of mind and outlook, she had started too late to have a truly original artistic vision. But as an executant, as an interpreter of styles evolved by others, she was in the first rank.

Enormously industrious, she made money, and banished the ghost of the poverty-stricken years. In 1886, Guinness was turned into a joint stock company, and members of the Purser family were given the chance to get in on the ground floor. Sarah put in all she could spare of her savings, and in due course reaped her reward. She continued to invest on the Stock Exchange, almost always profitably. But in actual painting fees, she told a niece towards the end of her life, she estimated that she had earned more than thirty thousand pounds.

She was to die possessed of the largest fortune, it is safe to say, that any Irishwoman has ever amassed by her own unaided efforts. But "once poor, always poor"—there are some ghosts that can never be quite laid. The full extent of her benefactions, particularly to fellow-artists, will never be known; but in the small things of day-to-day she retained her little thrifty habits, travelling third-class, communicating by postcard, not being on the telephone. This was what showed on the surface, and it led to the unkind legend of Sarah Purser the miser, a legend fostered by those who had tried unsuccessfully to presume on her generosity.

Certainly, she had a quick eye for a sponger. But the person she was always hardest on was herself.

3

Sarah Purser had now attained to a recognised ideal of happiness: her work and pleasure were one. She painted portraits, made money by them, enlarged her experience of human nature and indulged her passion for talk. "You'd never make a portrait painter," she later told one of her stained-glass artists, "because you can't paint and talk at the same time." She acquired the reputation of being the wittiest woman in Dublin, and the young Susan Mitchell, who lived next door, would listen wistfully to the gales of laughter proceeding from Miss Purser's, and wonder if the title would ever descend to herself. (As in fact it did.)

It is sad that so few of Sarah's *bons mots* survive. The most famous, "Some men kiss and tell, but George Moore tells and doesn't kiss," has passed into the language and people now forget who uttered it.* Most of the other examples repeated to me sound uncivil rather than amusing; perhaps they needed Sarah's stinging delivery to set them off.

She could also afford to indulge her second passion, which was for travel. She went abroad each summer, usually to Italy, and on the way would stop with Lulu Breslau in Paris, thus keeping abreast of trends in continental painting. Her training at Julien's had at least enabled her to by-pass Pre-Raphaelitism; now she came to appreciate Impressionism, for Mlle Breslau had become a close friend of Degas, and Sarah was always quick to seize on what was new. This interest was one of the links between her and Edward Martyn, the wealthy Catholic landowner who was Lady Gregory's neighbour in the West of Ireland, and who was building up his own collection of Impressionist paintings. At a time when most English and Irish art-criticism was still hopelessly provincial, Sarah Purser and Edward Martyn were Europeans in their outlook and taste.

Her principal artist friends in Ireland at this time were the Yeats family, living in Rathgar, but spending most of their collective days at the studio J. B. Yeats rented at 7 Stephens Green. They all painted; even Willie in a desultory way was studying art. There could hardly be a character better calculated than old J. B. Yeats to drive Sarah Purser wild. Lovable, improvident, immensely talented, immovably obstinate and quite impervious, he could only paint if the sitter inspired him, and it sometimes seemed that a sitter had only to be solvent for inspiration to fly out of the window. But to retain a model who took his fancy, he would spend weeks or even months of unnecessary fiddling—and then complain loudly that his native land failed to appreciate him and that he could not meet his bills.

* George Moore, like Falstaff a wit himself and the constant cause of wit in others, likewise had the honour of inspiring one of Susan Mitchell's best epigrams. Writing of his father, she says: "George Henry Moore possessed a fine honesty and frankness which he bequeathed to his sons—the honesty to Maurice, the frankness to George."

All through the summer of 1886 he was painting a new friend of Willie's, the taking young poetess Katharine Tynan, who of course could not pay a penny and would get the picture free. She records that he was reproaching her for having cut her fringe, when Miss Purser came in and observed: "Why, if she hadn't cut her fringe since she has been sitting to you, Mr. Yeats, it would be at her feet by now." Innocent Miss Tynan saw in this a feminine championship of her hair-dressing, but it is more likely that it was another sortie in the unending campaign of scolding Mr. Yeats.

Scolding: the word recurs whenever people remember Sarah Purser. It is undeniable that she scolded a great deal in her life; equally, that she had plenty of cause. Old Mr. Yeats represented in its extreme form that tendency to fecklessness, procrastination, and talk instead of action which has wasted so much talent in a city so lavishly endowed that it can, perhaps, afford the waste.

Sarah worshipped talent, and her desire to be of service to it was fundamentally humble, but where she loved, she chastised. The more gifted her victim, the more needful it was that he or she should be kept up to the mark. If only people would work regular hours, keep regular accounts, give themselves the trouble to advertise and market their wares, they might all of them be as prosperous as she was. There was nothing romantic about insolvency and muddle; she had learnt that for herself.

Sometimes, as in the case of old Mr. Yeats, her scoldings were so much waste of breath. But in the main, they got a great deal done. She was to the fine-art side of the Irish Renascence what Lady Gregory (though with much less temperamental zest for it) was to the dramatic: a constant goad. People stopped talking and wrote a play or painted a picture, if only to keep Lady Gregory and Miss Purser quiet.

Her closest affinity among the Yeatses was with the

schoolboy Jack, in whom she already discerned not only the major artistic talent of the family but also its shrewdest business head. In 1887 they all migrated back to London, J. B. Y. being the sort of optimist who readily believes that his fortunes may be improved by a change of scene without any corresponding change of behaviour; but in Bedford Park they were still the objects of Sarah Purser's anxious concern.

Jack had worked up a little connexion for himself in Dublin, drawing and selling menu and race cards, and Sarah, amid all her other preoccupations, made time to act as saleswoman for him and to get him further customers. There existed a charming series of letters from him to her, making plans for further sales, describing the American Exhibition at Earl's Court and the progress of Willie's first literary ventures, and illustrating his stories with marginal sketches far more sophisticated than the text. And they are not just the letters of a schoolboy who knows which side his bread is buttered. They treat her affectionately as confidant and equal. Sarah, for all her old-maidish ways, got on well with the young, and Jack Yeats knew that when he opened his whole mind to her, she would understand.

So much has been made of Sarah's "scoldings" that it is not always remembered how many and diverse people were deeply and permanently fond of her, relished her honesty and plain speaking, and relied on her staunchness as a friend. Edward Martyn, detester of the female sex in general, made an emphatic exception of her. Maud Gonne, who had been among her early sitters (a sugary full-length in the Municipal Gallery, with a pet monkey), wrote a letter of introduction to Mme de Sainte-Croix in Paris: "C'est un peintre de grand talent . . . elle n'a pas mes idées politiques mais cela n'importe pas que je l'aime beaucoup", and it was to Sarah's that Maud went to be nursed after she broke her arm falling off a cart during one of her speeches.

The minor poetess Jane Barlow appears to have had a sort of crush on Sarah, and wrote her a weekly letter for

years. To Sally Allgood she was "My darling Sarah—" in
letters written from Australian exile.

But nearest of all to her own heart, occupying the place
which might, had she been less sharp-featured and sharp-
tongued, have been filled jointly by a husband and a son,
was Lady Gregory's art-dealer nephew, Hugh Lane.

4

It was one of her major kindnesses which brought Lane
into her life. She and Martyn had long been of the opinion
that Nathaniel Hone was not receiving the recognition he
deserved; indeed, he had become so discouraged by Ireland's persistent neglect that he had ceased to exhibit, and
almost ceased to paint. She rented a small exhibition hall in
Stephens Green, and financed and arranged a showing of his
pictures and those of J. B. Yeats, doing everything, even down
to the compiling of the catalogue, herself.

The exhibition, of some forty canvases, lasted for ten days
in October-November of 1901, and for all its modest size it
attracted much attention and had important results. The
chief of these was the visit to it of Hugh Lane, who had made
his money by dealing in Old Masters, and had hitherto taken
very little interest in contemporary work. He was enormously enthusiastic over both artists, bought two Hone landscapes outright, and started the campaign of propaganda in
London and Paris art circles which was to secure for Hone a
European reputation. And from this show, too, arose his
dream of forming a personal collection of modern painting,
and then presenting it to Ireland, which would build a fitting
gallery to receive it.

Needless to say, this dream had Sarah's warm approval,

and she was to be Lane's principal collaborator in trying to realise it during the next fourteen years. She became correspondingly jealous of his other main supporter, his aunt Lady Gregory. Sarah was the staunchest of champions, but where she extended her championship, she liked to have a clear field.

The exhibition's consequences for J. B. Yeats were also better than even Sarah can have hoped. Lane gave him a series of commissions to paint the people who were bringing about the Irish Renascence, portraits which would form the nucleus of his Gallery of Modern Art when it should be attained. So the Yeats clan re-crossed the sea, and Mr. Yeats, being now provided with a variety of sympathetic sitters, got down to his task with real application and produced the enchanting set of likenesses which put Ireland almost as much in Hugh Lane's debt as do the Lane Pictures themselves. They included Lady Gregory, his son, both Fays, A. E., Horace Plunkett, Professor Dowden, Miss Horniman, Maire nic Shiubhlaigh, and J. M. Synge.

Then, inevitably, he quarrelled with Lane, and others had to be called in to complete the series, among them Orpen and Sarah Purser. Her two male portraits, of Martyn and of Douglas Hyde, show once again that her gift was for capturing character rather than for creating a work of pure art. They are not great portraits, but they have immediacy and freshness—Hyde with his branch of golden apples, Martyn as if about to sneeze. But with the two Allgood girls she failed, just as she had failed with Maud Gonne. It was not that they lacked either beauty or strong character; but for Sarah, there must be an intellectual quality in the sitter, if she was to give of her best.

For this reason she was happier painting men than women, but when an intellectual woman came her way she could show great sensibility. There is, for instance, her lovely portrait of her friend Jane Barlow in the National Gallery of Ireland; or her portrait of her niece Olive, the first girl to take First Class Honours and win a Gold Medal at Trinity. The darkly brooding young face above the sombre velvet dress seems to epitomise the feminist struggle in the early 20th century.

But the black dress, it appears, was just a fortunate fluke. "My best ball-dress was white," Miss Olive Purser recalls, "and I said: 'You needn't imagine, Aunt Sarah, that I'm going to wear it in your dirty old studio.' And so she lent me one of hers."

5

All through the '90's, Edward Martyn had been writing and speaking against the low standard of ecclesiastical architecture and ornament in Ireland; a fact brought sharply home to him when he wished to fill his parish church with stained glass, and found that his choice lay between the factory-made horrors—"oil paintings on glass"—of Birmingham and the even worse styles of Munich. He made several very active converts, among them the sculptor John Hughes, and Sarah. She, characteristically, was particularly annoyed to think of all the good business going out of Ireland, that might profitably be done at home.

To state, therefore, as Martyn later did in an often-quoted essay, that he "suggested" to Sarah the founding of a stained-glass workshop, and that "at first she was inclined to jib", may in all innocence do her rather less than justice. The idea had been in her mind for years, and if she "jibbed", it was doubtless at the prospect of financing all by herself what was bound to prove a costly experiment at first. The rich are, however, well-placed to give advice to their own kind, and Martyn would easily be able to convince her that his own fortune, though large, was already sufficiently engaged by his support of the theatrical and musical revivals, and of the new Roman Catholic cathedral being built in his home town of Loughrea.

Martyn was adviser to successive enlightened Bishops of Clonfert in the decoration of this remarkable building. (The see of Clonfert is an ancient one, but its tiny cathedral, in a village twenty miles east of Loughrea, had passed from Roman Catholic hands at the time of the Reformation.) He saw Loughrea Cathedral as the spearhead in his campaign to root out what he called "the foreign art commercial traveller", and to bring back a genuine artistic revival, based on Ireland's Celtic and Norman traditions. The artistic talent was there, he felt sure, but the need was for training-schools and workshops—and for the reform of taste that would accept the things they produced.

The chance came when the Dublin Metropolitan College of Art was removed from London control and placed under that of the newly-formed Department of Irish Agriculture, of which the secretary was the distinguished civil servant T. P. Gill. Edward and Sarah went to work on Gill, impressing on him the importance of including in the curriculum those arts chiefly needed for the decoration of churches —metal-work, enamelling, mosaic, embroidery, tapestry, and above all stained glass.

They visited the studio of Christopher Whall, almost the only man in England doing creative work in stained glass (he is well represented in Canterbury Cathedral). It was to Whall that Edward had turned for the first of his parish church windows, and they found in him a generous and disinterested counsellor. He was entirely sympathetic to the establishing of a native Irish stained-glass workshop, and promised them his favourite pupil A. E. Childe, as instructor and technician, provided that an adequate livelihood could be guaranteed.

Sarah painted Gill's portrait—he was another of those

long, lanky, intelligent sitters she adored—and improved the hours of the sittings by propaganda. If, she suggested, he would employ Childe part-time as stained-glass teacher at the School of Art, she on her side would make him manager and principal artist of her proposed workshop, which would co-operate with the School, and give employment to the best of its pupils as they qualified.

The bargain was clinched—it seems likely, from the affectionate tone of Gill's speech at the Tower's jubilee, that he did not need much persuading—and Sarah set about looking for her site. She found it at 24 Upper Pembroke Street, within a few hundred yards of Stephens Green. Dublin is much less thick on the ground than it appears from the streets, and behind its Georgian façades there are often large spaces, where sheds, workshops, wood-yards or hen-houses have insinuated themselves among the gardens. Or the whole façade may be broken to allow space for some grandee's pleasance. In Upper Pembroke Street there were two tennis courts; these Sarah secured, and on them built her glass works, then visible from the road. Now the frontage has been filled in, and one penetrates to the works through a tunnel beneath the houses.

She found for the little building a lovely name, taken from an old Irish legend: An Tur Gloine (pronounced Glinna), the Tower of Glass.

The reality was severely functional, and not at all the shimmering edifice the name suggests. But it provided what was necessary: a big, light studio, a small office, a workshop with benches for the glaziers, a gas-fired furnace. It met with the approval of Childe, and of the other English import, a Cockney glazier called Charlie Williams, with an accent so thick that at first nobody could understand a word he said. The second glazier, Tommy Kinsella, was an amusing boy from the Dublin slums, who had sold newspapers and was passionately interested in the theatre.

The workshop was ready by January of 1903, and opened

with a modest celebration. "Some friends, Mr. Hughes the sculptor was one of them, came as it were to see us off," Sarah recalled. "The shop was quite new, and oh, so cold! We gathered round the kiln and drank champagne out of teacups—it didn't taste very well, and we betook ourselves to the teapot."

At first Childe did most of the work, Sarah supplying an occasional cartoon—she has stated that she never did any actual glass painting. Childe's first important commission was for the three apse windows at Loughrea, which show him to be a fine technician, well ahead of his time, though too much imbued with Pre-Raphaelitism. But above all he was an excellent instructor, able to instil the "fourteen processes" into the heads of young artists with a genuine feeling for the medium, and to draw out of them much better work than he could do himself.

And already Sarah had had what was perhaps her greatest piece of luck—a genius was coming her way. Hughes had told her: "There's a young man at this moment crossing the Alps who draws a strong line." This was Michael Healy, son of an old Fenian, whose gifts had been recognised by the Dominicans; they had sent him to Rome to study for two years. On his return, Hughes steered him into Childe's classes at the School of Art, and being already artistically mature, he realised that in glass he had found his true medium. He swiftly mastered the technique, and executed his first window for Loughrea, the small St. Simeon in the baptistry, in 1904. Henceforward his entire career was passed at the Tower of Glass, and his Loughrea windows, the last of them completed in 1940, are a glittering screen upon which one may read the story of his unfolding genius.

Kitty O'Brien from Ennis, who had gone to the School of Art to study painting under Orpen and had been attracted to Childe's classes, was the first woman to join the staff; she was followed by Wilhelmina Geddes from Ulster, Ethel Rhind, who specialised in mosaic, Hubert MacGoldrick, another whose entire career was to pass at the Tower (he retired in 1944), and Beatrice Elvery. There were always more students knocking at the door than the Works could accommodate, and it was Sarah's grief that she had to turn so much promising young talent away.

Her part, it must be emphasised, was entirely disinterested. She had no ambition to paint stained glass herself, and she never made a penny of profit from the Tower. She did expect to have her capital repaid, and eventually it was, but the immense amount of time she put into the running of the business was given free. She was its principal commercial traveller, never lost an opportunity of pushing her artists, and on a railway journey would choose a carriage already occupied by a minister of religion, produce her pamphlets, and urge upon him the desirability of having artist-designed Irish stained glass in his church.

What, in effect, she had provided was an environment in which the artists could express themselves, and the apparatus enabling them to do so. As she explained in her speech at the jubilee celebrations, in an ordinary commercial glass workshop, a window would be standardised and divided up among several employees, who each drew and painted a part to sample.

"Now *we* hold that each window should be in all its artistic parts the work of one individual artist, the glass chosen and painted by the same mind and hand that made the design, and drew the cartoon, in fact a bit of stained glass should be a work of free art as much as any other painting or picture. Thus with us, each person gets a window or mosaic panel to do, and does it alone all through, according to his own ideas. The co-operation goes no further than supplying the craft means to do this; for stained glass, which Mr. Chesterton calls 'the thing that is more intoxicating than all the wines of the world,' is unluckily the least handy of the fine arts to make.

"You cannot do it in a romantic studio with silk cushions,

but must work in a grubby workshop, and must have kilns, and a large stock of glass and lead, etc., and someone to cut and glaze for you. All this is troublesome and expensive, and it is obvious no young artist uncertain of his orders could embark on it."

With her instinct for talent, she chose the right artists, and she left their work alone. Herself a working painter, she had none of that itch to interfere which caused Miss Horniman to become such a trial to the creative people in the Abbey Theatre. She respected her team, and was somewhat in awe of Healy and Geddes, the two most talented, both of them brooding introverts. It was only on matters of conduct and discipline that she endeavoured from time to time to assert her authority, and to remind them that this was a business and it ought to be businesslike. And once again, from what Beatrice Elvery and Kitty O'Brien remember of the Tower in its early days, she had reason good.

When there was a pressure of work, Charlie Williams and Tommy Kinsella worked like demons; at other times they played games with a ball of rolled-up newspaper, and studied racing form. The artists drifted in and out, nobody exercising any control except Childe, who was only there part-time. Wilhelmina Geddes, delicate and arthritic, worked when she felt equal to it, and Healy would give far more time to a window than its price could subsequently justify. Sarah would burst in at intervals, ginger everyone up, reduce somebody to tears, and depart knowing full well that they fell back into their old ways immediately. A memorandum shows her endeavouring to supply a form of remote control:

To the artists. I have done everything I could both by persuasion and by losing my temper to induce you to do what I feel is only due to your clients and to the Works. Things have got so go as you please in all departments, and it is hard to keep the time workers up to their hours when the artists often show so little energy and promptness. Instead of coming in at 12 and 1 to do the painting I must ask you all to be there ready to work at 10.15. It is not at all fair that the fag end of your days should be given to the work you earn your living by. I shall leave a book in which I shall ask you to enter every day your names and the hour.

Needless to say, this clocking-in scheme got her nowhere, except, perhaps, to complete the exacerbation of Miss Geddes. Of all the talents gathered under her roof, those of Healy and Geddes were nearest to Sarah's heart. But in the end Geddes could endure her no longer, and left to continue her career in London.

But the rest acknowledged freely their debt to Sarah Purser. They knew that she would stand by them in any adversity, and that it was her money, energy and salesmanship that made their work possible. They received from her constant kindnesses; trips abroad were financed, so that they could study old French and Italian glass, and also keep abreast of new developments. Kitty O'Brien recalls being taken abroad three times, and Beatrice Elvery similarly remembers a tour of English cathedrals and churches, ending at Tewkesbury, where Sarah looked for Purser ancestors.

And after any row, little presents of fruit or flowers would arrive. "She never actually apologised," one is told, but even that is not quite true, as is proved by this touching note scrawled right at the end of her life. (The dispute had been over an insubordinate craftsman.)

Dear Miss O'Brien,

What a beast I was—and I full of admiration for your energy and good sense and the way you are handling this just horrid situation—and I hate myself for keeping always rubbing in my beastly money—try to excuse me, and keep C. on, say for the present—until Mr. Healy's window is done, or Hittler [*sic*] takes us over to protect. I will send the £12 tomorrow. Please forgive, yours, S. H. P.

And should any attack be made on the team from outside, Sarah was prepared to defend them like a dragon. She had assembled their talents with skill, and though quite as eager as Martyn to raise the general standard of stained glass, was at the same time determined to attract all the orders she could, and not frighten clients away. Those with the finest taste, treasures like Archbishop Healy and Cardinal O'Donnell, were led towards Michael Healy, Wilhelmina Geddes or Hubert MacGoldrick; Childe could please the more conventional; the gentle, very "Irish" talent of Kitty O'Brien was ideally suited to the simplicity of village churches; while Beatrice Elvery, now, as Lady Glenavy, one of Ireland's most distinguished painters in oils, cheerfully admits that her longing was always for that medium, and that she did stained glass to fill in the time. Her technique was as sound as that of all Childe's pupils, but she saw no reason why customers should not have what pleased them best.

This gave rise to one of Sarah Purser's most Homeric and amusing rows. The Abbey Theatre set were, of course, among her supporters, and one of her first commissions had been the stained glass for the Abbey vestibule. The nuns at Lady Gregory's home town of Gort wanted stained glass for their convent chapel, and Lady Gregory guided them to An Tur Gloine. They arrived bearing a picture which they wanted copied exactly in glass, and Sarah allotted it to young Miss Elvery to execute.

Soon afterwards, Yeats and Lady Gregory looked in at the workshop, perceived the cartoon for the window upon a drawing-table, and departed horrified; and in the next issue of *Samhain*, Yeats's "occasional publication", there was an article by him deploring that Miss Purser's Stained Glass Works were going the way of all artistic ventures in Ireland, and having begun with the highest standards and ideals, were rapidly descending to the lowest. Sarah read it, and next day, Yeats received a Purser broadside:

Dear Willie,

I have only just seen your last Samhain. I have never

objected to criticism of my publickly [*sic*] shown work, but to publish an entirely garbled and in most ways fake account of what you may have seen when, in my absence, you came uninvited to my private place of business, and also to attribute to me motives which I had to yourself denied being mine—goes, I consider, beyond the limits of decent manners, and is conduct which would make all social intercourse impossible.

Of course Yeats apologised; he genuinely relished Sarah Purser, and appreciated both what she had done for his family and what she was trying to do for Irish art. And of course he was forgiven; it was not in Sarah to bear lasting enmity towards a Yeats.

But Lady Gregory was not. The incident only deepened the feeling of dislike that Sarah already had for Hugh Lane's favourite aunt. "I don't interfere with your Abbey Theatre, you keep off my glass works," she is said to have observed next time they met. Poor Lady Gregory must have been heartily sorry she had not allowed the nuns of Gort to order their window through a catalogue from Birmingham.

6

It is a reproach to several distinguished Dublin art historians—or perhaps to their publishers—that the critical history of An Tur Gloine and its achievement has not yet been written. Perhaps another Sarah Purser is needed, to scold them into doing it.

The omission does, however, mean that one can enjoy the excitement of discovering masterpieces for oneself, and a rewarding holiday could be spent hunting them through Ireland—or through England, and, if funds permitted, across the seas. For though Ireland is the country richest in glass from the Tower, it cannot be said that Edward and Sarah's dream of a country filled with beautiful churches was realised, and the majority of customers continued to prefer the garish and the factory-made. Sarah was therefore frequently obliged to look overseas for commissions to keep her artists going.

The outstanding merit of the Tower artists was to have returned to the mediaeval tradition of "thinking in glass"— a tradition which, had it not been for Cromwell and his vandals, could probably have been studied as richly in Ireland as in France. The Tower's work is informed from first to last by an understanding of the material, so that whatever the subject, one feels it could not have been expressed in any other medium. They were the first corporate body of artists to revive the mediaeval craft outlook in glass, and even today, when we are at last beginning to get away from the notion that a stained-glass window should look like an enlarged colour-photograph, it is possible to claim that theirs is still the most important achievement in glass of modern times.

They were specifically Irish artists, reaching back for their inspiration to such masterpieces as the Ardagh Chalice and the Cross of Cong; yet the best of their output escapes the taint of provincialism and can stand up to European scrutiny. And this (granted that Healy and Evie Hone had had continental training) was due in no small part to Sarah's alert and cosmopolitan outlook, and to the generosity whereby she made it possible for them to travel and observe.

And they brought to the predominantly religious art of stained glass a passionate piety; it might be said of all of them, as it was of Kitty O'Brien at her death, that their labours seemed to be an extension of their prayers. Healy and MacGoldrick devout Catholics, Evie Hone a Catholic convert, Kitty O'Brien a disciplined High Anglican, Wilhelmina Geddes a Presbyterian—their faiths were as varied as their temperaments. Sarah herself, although officially Protestant, was not a pious woman. Her religion was art, and her shafts of sarcasm did not spare religious vagaries which seemed to her to be getting in its way. (That princes of the Hierarchy like Archbishop Healy remained so fond of her is a tribute not only to their Christian forbearance but to their sense of humour.) Nevertheless, when it came to choosing artists for the Tower, her flair guided her to the outlook, as well as the talent, that would best serve her stained-glass crusade.

With so much in common, the painters yet show widely differing artistic personalities, and it is curious that the two most monumental should have been women, Geddes and Hone. Healy and Hone, the acknowledged geniuses, were close friends and yet are poles apart, Healy drawing his principal inspiration from the Florentine Renascence, while Hone is Gothic and French.

Most of Michael Healy's work is in Ireland, Loughrea Cathedral forming virtually a gallery of his development. There are also exceptionally fine windows by him in Letter-kenny Cathedral and in the Augustinian Priory church in Dublin. He was the inventor of the "aciding" process, which gives to even the deepest colours a transparent, jewel-like glitter; a process vulgarised by some of his imitators, but which in his hands emphasises the complicated, yet per-fectly ordered, richness of the design.

Loughrea makes a tremendous impact, particularly at evening, when the setting sun shines through his two great three-light windows, the Ascension and the Last Judgement. Before this latter, his last work, one stands transfixed. From the upturned faces of the damned in hell to the enthroned Figure, it seems to surge upward in a great pyramidal movement, humanity's anguish and striving and need for mercy caught and sublimated in a thousand jewelled facets of glass.

If Healy is still imperfectly appreciated, Wilhelmina

Geddes is so nearly forgotten that her finest window, the Crucifixion in St. Luke's, Wallsend, was attributed in a recent Northumberland guidebook to Evie Hone. And indeed they have affinities: Geddes too is "Gothic", and Evie studied with her for a time in London. Geddes was mistress of a particularly beautiful, mellow, Old Master colouring, making great use of yellow and umber, and her figures have an elongated, El Greco stylisation. There are small windows by her in the Protestant church of St. Anne's, Dawson Street, in Dublin, and an important window in St. Bartholomew, Ottawa, erected by the Duke of Connaught in memory of members of his Canadian staff who died during the First World War.

A pilgrimage to Wallsend to view the Geddes masterpiece would be doubly rewarding, for this Tyneside town, not commonly regarded as a beauty spot, is richer than any other in England in glass from An Tur. This happy result was due to the presence in it of two influential Irish clerics, Canon C. E. Osborne, brother of Sarah's friend the painter Walter Osborne, who was rector of St. Peter's, Wallsend, from 1906 to 1936, and Canon T. W. Allen, vicar of the daughter church of St. Luke's.

St. Luke's has the Geddes Crucifixion, which has been called "the finest window north of the Alps", and St. Peter's has five smaller windows, three by Healy, one by MacGoldrick and one by Ethel Rhind.

Canon Frank Hurst, then a young curate and later Rector, recalls the visits of Sarah to Wallsend, the mixture of awe and enthusiasm that she inspired, and the puzzlement of congregations as the Irish windows went up, so different from the Victorian sentimentalities to which they were accustomed. But that was long ago, and today the people of Wallsend are aware of their good fortune in possessing so much beauty amid the grime of Tyneside, and are thankful for the miracle which preserved it to them through all the bombings of the last war.

The benign Irish saints of Kitty O'Brien, often standing above miniature landscapes (a favourite device with her teacher, Childe), are the movement's nearest approach to folk-art, and have close affinities with the banners and other embroideries executed for Loughrea by Lily Yeats and her Cuala Industries. Miss O'Brien, the last active member of the group, was working almost up to her death in July of 1963, and left unfinished her last commission, which was from President de Valera for two windows in the private chapel of the presidential lodge.

Hubert MacGoldrick is recognised as Healy's successor, akin, but not an imitator, an artist of great sensibility and religious feeling. He is represented by a Sacred Heart window at Loughrea, by a Resurrection in the mortuary chapel at Aughrim Street, Dublin, and by a very beautiful Baptism in Jordan in one of the Cork churches, but his most important work is in Singapore Cathedral. Ethel Rhind, though she did glass painting, specialised in mosaic. Her Stations of the Cross at Loughrea, framed in pale green Connemara marble so that they seem to grow out of the walls, have great dignity and pathos. The naturalism demanded by the terrible story is tempered by the slight stylisation of the medium, and one feels that she has solved a problem which baffled many of the Old Masters.

The last and best-known recruit to the Tower, Evie Hone, was like Healy a mature artist before she joined it in 1933, having been rejected by Sarah nine years before. (This was Sarah's one serious failure in artistic appreciation, to which I will return.) Evie Hone had studied with Gleizes, one of the minor Cubists; she had been influenced by Lhote and Picasso, and particularly by Rouault, whose painting is already so nearly "stained glass". She brought entirely new currents of feeling and expression into the Dublin of the 1930's, creating at first something of an uproar. Only when her great abstract window "My Four Green Fields" was exhibited at the New York World's Fair of 1938 did Irishmen concede that Kathleen ni Houlihan could be symbolised more dynamically than by a colleen in a shawl.

Evie Hone is already a contemporary, and for this reason it is perhaps easier for us to appreciate her work than that of Healy or Geddes, which is just at a remove to make elements in it seem dated. Yet like them she has very Irish grass-roots, and from her contact with them as colleagues, and from her study of early Irish crosses and carvings, she derived elements of great strength and tenderness. The parallel between her largest window, the Crucifixion in Eton College Chapel, and Geddes's Crucifixion at Wallsend is close.

In Ireland, she has important work at Loughrea; at Clongowes Wood College chapel (where she completed a commission left unfinished by Healy at his death); at Black-rock and Greystones; at Ardara, County Donegal. "My Four Green Fields", having been packed away in crates for nearly twenty years, was finally re-erected in the new offices of the Passenger Bureau of Coras Iompair Eireann (the National Transport Company) in O'Connell Street, Dublin, which thereby became one of the most visually distinguished information centres in the world. In England, besides the Eton window, her Crucifixion in the parish church of Downe, Kent, should be seen.

A memorial exhibition of Evie Hone's work, held in Dublin in 1958, was brought to London by the Arts Council the following year. Given the difficulty of displaying stained glass, or even effective colour-transparency reproductions of it, this display was something of an eye-opener to the English art world. Perhaps, one day, a complete retrospective exhibition of An Tur Gloine will permit a fuller idea of the riches and beauty that came out of Sarah Purser's ramshackle little workshop, tucked away in a Dublin back-yard.

7

Sarah's work for the Tower was not allowed to interfere with her own career as a portraitist, and the fact of being a practising painter probably made her a better studio director, just as the fact of being a practising dramatist enabled Lady Gregory to be a fully creative director at the Abbey.

Old Mrs. Purser having died in 1901, Sarah had moved into the house at the canal end of Harcourt Terrace, that delectable corner of Regency Dublin; it had a stable which she converted into a studio. This remains, though no longer serving the purpose today. She could be more choosy now over her sitters, paint fewer society women, and concentrate on her favourites, clever men; and with two brothers professors at Trinity, her access to supplies of clever men was facilitated. Many of her Trinity portraits have real distinction; her study of John Kells Ingram, the Professor of Political Economy, is probably the best.

She spent a great deal of her time in seconding Hugh Lane's efforts to get Dublin a gallery of modern art. Between them they browbeat the Corporation into renting a house in Harcourt Street, as temporary home for the nucleus of a collection, most of it given by Lane himself. It was opened on June 20th, 1908, but like all makeshifts it had serious deficiencies. For one thing, the buildings constituted a fire risk; and the two friends could not be content with anything less than a specially erected gallery, Lane making the outright gift of his pictures contingent on the Corporation doing its share.

At 6 Harcourt Street, many Dublin eyes were opened

for the first time to the glories of French Impressionist painting; but the city as a whole was less than enthusiastic about Mr. Lane and his foreign art. There ensued a long and wearisome bickering between Lane and the Corporation, sites and plans for a Gallery being constantly proposed and as constantly rejected; until, as the whole world had cause to know later on, Lane grew exasperated, withdrew his gift, lent it to the Tate Gallery in London, and altered his will. Lady Gregory in her *Life* of her nephew says very little about Sarah Purser's part in the fight for a gallery; but then Lady Gregory had had a good deal to put up with from Sarah's jealous dislike, and this sin of omission is a perhaps understandable revenge.

There is an amusing glimpse of Sarah, as usual standing no nonsense, in a letter of Yeats next year. "I went to Paris for a few days before I came here [Burren] and met Sarah Purser at Maud Gonne's. She was as characteristic as ever, as like herself as a John drawing. Maud Gonne had a cage full of canaries and the birds were all singing. Sarah Purser began lunch by saying 'What a noise! I'd like to have my lunch in the kitchen!'" (To J. B. Yeats, July 17th, 1909.)

The houses in Harcourt Terrace have spacious rooms, but even so there was insufficient scope to feed Sarah's hunger for good company. In 1911 she and her unmarried brother John Mallet Purser, the Regius Professor of Medicine, together took a long lease of Mespil House, on the further side of the canal. Mespil was an 18th-century mansion, famed for its superb plaster ceilings, and standing in what almost amounted to a little park, with an artificial lake and stream. Though still only half a mile from the centre of the city, Sarah could now boast that she was the only woman in Dublin who could keep a cow on her front lawn.

The house's principal feature was the vast first-floor drawing-room, approached by a noble staircase; and here Sarah, holding an afternoon reception on the second Tuesday of each month, endeavoured to revive the glories of a salon in the Age of Elegance. She knew "all Dublin", having painted most of it; and "all Dublin" came. Came, moreover, to a refreshment of tea and cakes, for the parties were officially dry, though important male visitors might be led by a nephew to a hidden provision of drinks downstairs.

"Miss Purser's Second Tuesdays." became a Dublin institution, and a good many elderly people look back on them wistfully, remembering the beautiful staircase with the Orpen picture of gypsies at the top, the drawing-room with its Seurats and Vlamincks, the Empire couch and the big Japanese screen. The company might be anything from fifty to a hundred and fifty strong (small wonder that with numbers so uncertain, the sandwich fillings sometimes had to be spread a little thin), and if there were a visiting celebrity in Dublin, Miss Purser would probably have captured him or her, for her organisation was efficient. The Professor, a shy man, had no part in it, immuring himself in his study till everyone had gone, but nephews and nieces were dragooned into service. They too retain their memories of "Aunt Sarah's Days of Wrath", of her firm way with guests and conversations ("Now you two sit on that sofa and talk about golf"), and of her habit of landing them with the dull halves of married couples, usually, alas, the wives.

The mere possession of a large room could not have brought the clever and the witty to Sarah Purser's door. They came because her parties were good fun, and a triumph of her own personality. They came to savour her particular combination of kind heart and sharp tongue, to hear her deflate pomposity and expose pretence. Dublin dearly loves a debunking, and one never quite knew what Sarah would say next or on whom the blow might fall. One heard her lay one's enemies low, at the risk of being a victim oneself. One joked about it—though not, if one were wise, to her face. A young Dublin artist exhibited a cartoon of "Sarah Purser entertaining her Friends", which showed her as a whirling dervish, aiming her daggers at a cowering circle. Sarah threatened a libel action, and the cartoon was withdrawn.

The principal object of the receptions was to give pleasure, and Sarah with her dislike of humbug would not have pretended anything else. But they also performed a genuine cultural function. They were neutral ground, where Protestant and Catholic, "loyalist" and Nationalist, could meet; and they were feminine neutral ground, permitting women their share in the literary and artistic discussions which tended otherwise to be too much confined to male clubs and bars.

The main cause they furthered was that of art. Young painters who were Sarah's protégés were introduced to sitters and patrons; stained-glass commissions were canvassed for the Tower; the agitation for the gallery was never allowed to die down. And presently Sarah had the happiness of seeing relations between Dublin and her beloved Lane improve. He accepted the directorship of the National Gallery of Ireland, though refusing to take a penny of the salary; he wrote out the—unfortunately unwitnessed—codicil to his will which restored to Dublin his personal collection of pictures. Sarah herself was made a trustee of the National Gallery early in 1914, and her influence and authority were thereby increased.

Then came the war, and with it what was, perhaps, the most deeply felt sorrow of Sarah's personal life. Hugh Lane's strange, showy, quixotically generous career came to its end. He crossed to America to negotiate a big art deal, returned on the *Lusitania*, and went down with her on May 7th, 1915.

Thomas MacGreevy remembers Sarah calling at the National Gallery on business a little while later, and finding these rooms, so saturated with memories of her lost friend, more than she could bear. "Oh, my poor Lane," she said, "my poor Lane," and she put her head down on the desk and sobbed.

He claims he is the only person in Dublin who ever saw Sarah Purser cry.

8

Revolutionary politics were not Sarah's métier. She called herself a Protestant Unionist, but made it her business to keep on good terms with all who could further the progress of art. At the same time she was intelligent enough to be aware that the artistic resurgence itself had derived much of its impetus from the Nationalist one. She had painted past and present leaders of revolt, like Michael Davitt and Roger Casement, and had listened to their talk. This extract from a diary she kept in the week after the Easter Rising illustrates the ambivalence of her attitude, her championship of common-sense and business-as-usual conflicting with a sneaking sympathy for the heroic gesture and the resolute heart:

"Wednesday, 3rd May. Only a few stray shots since midnight, some of them no doubt those that ended three of the leaders. Pearse I had had some business dealing with, making him some lead lights and Miss Elvery doing him pictures when he first set up the school—but he has left no personal impression on me and I should not have recognised him if I saw him—I was once years ago at a pageant at the School when it was in Cullenswood. It was a very creditable and interesting performance. At the time we all thought it a very fine thing that there should be a Catholic *lay* school in Ireland, and we all looked sympathetically at the venture—but I don't suppose it could have succeeded even if managed in a business-like way which I fancy it never was.

"I am thankful that none of the people I am really acquainted with even or came much in contact with are among those who have risen except Con Markievicz, and I feel sorrier than I can say for her poor Mother—when one thinks

of the lovely child and young girl she was and how idolised
and spoilt and always so good hearted in her absurdities—
I did not think she would let herself be taken but am glad
at least to hear the histrionics of her kissing her revolver,
etc., denied. . . .

"John Griffiths and Elsie walked over and were sympathetic about the pictures. They had heard John MacNeill's
defection had prevented 1,500 Volunteers turning up which
may have made all the difference. If so he must sleep
uneasily. One would like to be inside a good many who were
very extreme physical force men and didn't come out. After
all everyone can't command their nerves and it was a tragic
absurdity all through—still they will never respect themselves again. . . .

"Things settling down again—we are trying to get the
shop going but are held up for want of gas.

"Crowds in the streets as naturally no one scarcely is at
work and really no air of depression at all. Came home
deadly tired having quarrelled with everyone and been
disagreeable to them at the shop over wages."

The passing reference to "the pictures" might in a lesser
woman have been an anguished cry, for the premises of the
Royal Hibernian Academy had been among the casualties of
Easter Week, and all her canvases in the spring exhibition
had been lost. One of them was a portrait of Molly Allgood
in the sea-green robes of Synge's Deirdre, said to have been
very beautiful—though I find it hard to credit that there was
enough sympathy between Sarah and that particular sitter
for real penetration into character.

The years of "the Troubles" were from the Purser viewpoint a total loss. Naturally Sarah welcomed the Treaty,
deplored the Civil War, and hailed the Cosgrave Government as restorers of peace and prosperity. She became a
personal friend of President Cosgrave, who was frequently
to be met with at her Second Tuesdays. The 1920's were
Mespil House's period of greatest influence, and Sarah made

two more notable contributions to the artistic life of her country, both of them bound up with her struggle to carry out the last wishes of Hugh Lane.

She and Lady Gregory to some extent buried the hatchet, and divided up the task between them, Lady Gregory concentrating on trying to get the Lane Pictures back from England, and Sarah on securing the Dublin gallery that was to house them. She even went so far as to suggest that Lady Gregory should join her on the Board of Trustees of the National Gallery of Ireland; and Lady Gregory, though she declined the honour, was touched and pleased.

In 1924, Sarah conceived the idea of forming a society of "Friends of the National Collections of Ireland", on the lines of the "Friends of Rembrandt" in Amsterdam and the "Friends of the Louvre" in Paris. Its primary purpose, as well as campaigning for the return of Lane's pictures, was to buy further continental paintings; there already existed a trust fund for the purchase of Irish art. The Society came into being at a meeting held at the temporary premises of the Royal Hibernian Academy on February 14th, and it has ever since maintained a steady flow of gifts to museums and galleries all over Ireland, Belfast included.

In 1928, the Friends under Sarah's leadership held a big public meeting to demand the return of the Lane Pictures, and this was followed by a public enquiry at the City Hall into the possibility of building a gallery. Then Sarah had another of her inspirations. Charlemont House, a magnificent Georgian mansion at the top of Parnell Square, had recently been vacated by the Registrar-General's department and stood empty. Why not, she suggested to Cosgrave, use it for the gallery, by keeping the façade as entrance hall and offices, and building out modern picture galleries into the big garden at the back?

Cosgrave agreed that the Government should present the building to Dublin Corporation, which was aghast at this Trojan gift. Where was the money to come from for reconditioning, enlargement, and salaries? And once again the answer was, largely through Sarah and her Friends.

The Dublin Municipal Gallery of Modern Art, one of the most attractive and dignified galleries in Europe, is Sarah Purser's creation more than any other person's, and remains her principal monument. So, for that matter, do its contents; the Lane Pictures, now shared with Britain by the compromise arrangement of 1959, are its principal glory, but it is also rich in Post-Impressionists bought chiefly with subscriptions from the Friends. It is likewise a national portrait gallery of the people who made the Renascence and the Republic, and that again is largely Sarah's doing; it was she who made it possible for J. B. Yeats, Orpen and the rest of them to get to work.

One's only regret is that her own contributions do not do justice to her talent; but perhaps that may be remedied in time. There are many distinguished portraits by her, still on private walls, which should find their way into the Municipal Gallery of Modern Art in the end.

9

Another gratifying celebration of this period was the jubilee of An Tur Gloine. A gathering at the Shelbourne Hotel on January 19th, 1928, was addressed by T. P. Gill, the workshop's "godfather", and then by Sarah herself, making what was positively her first public speech. That a woman so strong-minded and apt at expressing her opinions should never have expressed them from a platform before brings home to one how little Irishwomen were as yet accustomed to taking part in public life.

She acquitted herself gaily, paying tribute to the artists

("we have stuck together and not quarrelled too much"),
to the glaziers ("the same Mr. Williams and Mr. Kinsella
as were there in 1903 still cut and glaze for us in superior
fashion"), and to the long-suffering accountant ("I fear at
first he had a weary time, you would hear him sighing,
wherever is the balance of those three archangels?").
She explained that though the work had always been done
on a co-operative, profit-sharing basis, she was now turning
the Tower into a legal co-operative, and in future the artists
would own it between them. She only regretted that they
had come on the scene so late:

"Our grief is that we are not 125 years old instead of 25.
Think of the chance Ireland had then! *All* the Catholic
churches and great ecclesiastical establishments to be built
through Ireland—almost all the Protestant churches either
to be built or remodelled, and all the glass, altars, furnishings
of all sorts to be got.

"A people full of genuine piety, ready out of their poverty
to give unstintingly, and gifted in the most remarkable way
for decorative and manipulative art. Well, we know the
result—if only the architects and Schools of Art and the
clergy had joined hands and worked up to this enormous
demand Ireland would undoubtedly now be the greatest
centre of religious art in the world. No other Nation was in
quite the same fortunate position. It seems a simple idea to
grasp, but the usual Great Enchantment fell on us, and the
chance was lost, and in the matter of glass the current was
set so firmly towards Birmingham and Munich that most of
our energy has to go persuading people against bringing in a
poorer art than they could get here.

"It has been a bit disappointing that the Churches have
not been more generally enthusiastic in realising we were
doing their work, that we should have to look abroad for
orders, and to our sorrow discourage many obviously
talented young artists from joining us. But we have always
had staunch and excellent friends, some who ventured full

of faith to risk giving us windows before they had seen much of our output. They may be sure we remember them with fervent gratitude, for that is another of the drawbacks of glass, you can't do it like pictures *on chance*, it must be ordered. Still, we have held on, and have a lot of work to our account, our last order is numbered 637 in our books. . . ."

Then she took occasion to clear up a point which had been troubling her honest heart:

"I myself, though I hope I am some judge of glass, am not a stained-glass worker in the sense we give to the work. My only output is a tiny window in the porch at Loughrea, something in the nature of a curiosity. I designed, as Mr. Gill kindly remembered, some of our early windows, but though the real glass artists obligingly painted them, we never found it satisfactory. Now I would not have troubled you with these personal matters only that it is greatly on my mind to correct a misapprehension I very often come upon, and which annoys me very much—that the artists in 24 Pembroke Street are in some way my pupils and under my directions. This, of course, is entirely not so. They are each born with their own imagination and sense of colour, and learned to draw before specialising in stained glass, and have each developed their techniques on lines of their own, for handling the material, and are not interfered with by anybody. And as far as possible in this rather confusing business, they get the credit or the blame personally for their work."

That is Sarah at her generous best. It is sad to have to record that the 1920's also witnessed her one serious failure in artistic patronage, the case of Evie Hone. It was a personal rather than an aesthetic failure, for when in 1924 Evie Hone and Mainie Jellett held the joint exhibition of paintings which introduced Cubism to an outraged Dublin, Sarah was certainly not among the outraged. She had been taking Cubism in her Parisian stride for years.

F

Evie Hone presented herself at the Tower with cartoons for three small stained-glass panels and expected to be admitted; this, it would seem, was her crime. All the Tower artists, no matter what their previous achievements in painting, had taken a course of technical training at the School of Art under Childe. Sarah told Evie roundly she must do the same, and quite possibly she sounded more discouraging than she had intended.

But Evie had already outgrown Childe. She attended his classes briefly, decided he had nothing to teach her, and went back to London, where she persuaded Wilhelmina Geddes to take her as a pupil, and where she converted the cartoons into her first pieces of stained glass in Miss Geddes's kiln. She went on to Roland Holst in Amsterdam, famous both as stained-glass artist and as teacher, and after that she bided her time, painting in oil and gouache, and returning for frequent "refresher courses" with Gleizes in Paris. Thus nine years of her all too short career were, if not exactly wasted, at least unfruitful as far as stained glass was concerned.

A similar myopia afflicted the directorate of the Abbey Theatre when it rejected Sean O'Casey's play *The Silver Tassie*, but Yeats and Lady Gregory had less excuse than Sarah, for O'Casey had already proved to them that he was a dramatist of great drawing-power; whereas it needed the eye of faith to perceive the genius behind Evie Hone's small sketches. But it was Sarah's business to possess such a eye—and it appears that she did not forgive herself for the failure, nor Evie either.

In 1933, with a greatly enhanced reputation, Evie again knocked at the Tower door. By now she could prove that there were clients ready with commissions; Sarah was never one to turn work away, and she was admitted. Nor did it take Sarah long to appreciate the magnitude and originality of her talent, but between that and liking her as a person there was a gulf. Evie Hone, gentle, dedicated, and with that profound humility which does sometimes accompany real greatness, was almost a saint. Sarah was no saint, and this relationship begun on the wrong footing was not one of which she could make a success.

There was also an element of jealousy over Healy. Evie worked in the next bay to him and learnt much from him, and between the two withdrawn spirits there sprang up a close understanding; he may also have influenced her religious life and her conversion. Had it not been for Healy's death in 1940, the two artists would probably have left the Tower and set up on their own.

But if Evie had a good deal to forgive Sarah, she also had much for which to feel grateful. Genius knows what it needs, and she needed An Tur Gloine, its atmosphere, its comradeship, its Irishness. She could easily have got herself accepted by a London or Paris glassworks, and she would not. Once safely established at 24 Upper Pembroke Street, with Michael Healy for her friend, and Tommy Kinsella, the cheerful racing specialist, to do her glazing, she went ahead and produced works of ever-increasing beauty and power. An Tur made her career possible, and Sarah made An Tur. In this sense it is true to say that without Sarah Purser there would have been no Evie Hone.

10

When de Valera made his dramatic return to power in 1932, Sarah's days of public influence were over. She had regarded the Cosgrave Government as a fixture, and had neglected to take her customary precaution of making contact with all parties. Ironically enough, it was the new President who opened the Municipal Gallery in 1934; but she was never able to interest him in the cause of art as she had interested Mr. Cosgrave. The loss was Ireland's.

However, she was now in her mid-eighties, and might justly consider that she had performed her share of public service. And incredibly, she continued to paint, and to paint better than ever. These last portraits—Jack Yeats, James MacNeill, C. P. Curran, Thomas MacGreevy among them— were not done for money, but for love of good talk and good company. It was an honour to be invited by Miss Purser to sit, and the sitter was presented with his picture afterwards. He probably received a few scoldings and home-truths by the way, and that was an honour too. "You're not a *bon morceau* like Sir John Griffiths," she grumbled to MacGreevy, "I can't get your bones." (Respectfully considering the patrician features of the former Director of Ireland's National Gallery, one concludes that in this instance Miss Purser was just being captious.)

These late pictures have never been exhibited. If someone in Dublin would do for Sarah Purser what she in her lifetime did for her contemporaries, and organise a complete retro- spective exhibition, I believe she would emerge as a far more considerable artist than has been at all realised.

Active, healthy, indomitable, she was a little old woman in appearance, but in nothing else. She routed a burglar with her tongue ("How dare you come into a lady's bedroom?" she demanded, and being a modest Irish burglar, he fled at once). At eighty-nine she insisted that Oliver Gogarty should take her up in his private aeroplane to inspect the roof of Mespil House. They circled it three times and then she wrote a letter of complaint to her landlord, Sir Almroth Wright— who replied that her lease had run out ten years before and he hadn't had the heart to tell her so.

She remained both business-like and generous, expected to be repaid when she had made a loan, and then, as likely as not, would put the cheque into the fire. And she never lost her feeling for new trends in art. A student of those years, taken to a Second Tuesday, expected to find this venerable person harking back to past glories; but she wanted to discuss with him Picasso and Matisse.

She was the oldest of the little group who made the Irish Renascence, and she outlived most of them. She lived on into the world of the Second War, and very nearly into the atomic age. The war cut her off from her foreign travel, but she was still able to pass active summers on the west coast. She was about to leave for her favourite Mayo hotel in July of 1943 when she suffered a slight stroke.

"She was killed by a stamp," people tell you, and like so much of her legend it has an element of truth. The stamp was issued in honour of her old friend and sitter Douglas Hyde, first President of Ireland. It used a poor portrait in a feeble design, and she flew into one of her famous rages, which brought the seizure on.

She seemed to recover, and was only with difficulty dissuaded by her family from making the journey to Mayo. "If I can sit in a chair," she protested, "I can sit in a railway carriage." But a fortnight later (August 7th, 1943) she was dead.

She died on a Saturday, and was buried on the following Tuesday. People felt that they were saying goodbye to an epoch, and an even larger company followed her coffin than had thronged the drawing-room of Mespil House. Only when the arrangements for the funeral were completed did the family suddenly realise that it would be a Second Tuesday.

Sarah Henrietta Purser entertained her circle to the last.

SOURCES:

An Tur Gloine: Jubilee pamphlet, 1928.
Stella Frost, ed.: *A Tribute to Evie Hone and Mainie Jellett*. Dublin, Browne & Nolan, 1957.

Lady Gregory: *Hugh Lane's Life and Achievements, with some Account of the Dublin Galleries.* London, John Murray, 1921.

Lady Gregory: *Journals*, edited by Lennox Robinson. London, Putnam, 1946.

Denis Gwynn: *Edward Martyn and the Irish Revival.* London, Cape, 1930.

Recollections of Miss Olive Purser, Mrs. Parker, Professor and Mrs. John Purser, the late Kitty O'Brien, the late Diarmuid Coffey, Mr. C. P. Curran, Beatrice Lady Glenavy, Dr. Thomas MacGreevy, Canon Frank Hurst, Mr. John F. O'Kelly, Mrs. W. E. Phillips, Miss Mary Swanzy.

Sally and Molly:

SARA ALLGOOD and MAIRE O'NEILL

I

THAT THE art of acting is ephemeral is a truism which the inventions of sound and film recording have done little to disprove. The old films flicker, the gestures, the clothes, the hairdressing are dated and grotesque. The old recordings wheeze and boom, and exude a rich aroma of ham.

A player can still only survive in legend, and only a handful of them have contrived to do so. But Sara Allgood and her sister Maire O'Neill are of the company. No one who saw them act has ever forgotten them, and no one who acted with them ever seems to have been quite so impressed by any other fellow-performers. "The two finest actresses I ever saw", Maureen Delany told me shortly before her death. And much the same tribute was paid recently by the veteran Abbey actors Mr. Arthur Shields and Mr. J. M. Kerrigan, interviewed in Hollywood.

The legend of Sally and Molly Allgood is the more remarkable because both outlived, if not their talents, at any rate the scope allowed to them, and tailed away unhappily into bit-parts. Also, their years of triumph were in a theatre where most of the great parts (as in most theatres) were written for men. The Abbey produced many excellent male performers, who are now honoured names in the theatrical histories; but none of them possessed the quality of glamour.

This overworked word accurately describes the outstanding attribute of the Allgood sisters. They were magical; they cast a spell. Magic is, if not an essential, at any rate a highly valuable element in a creative theatre. Dramatists are inspired by it, audiences are held. The Abbey was primarily a dramatists' theatre, but Synge and Lady Gregory were directly influenced in their writing by the presence of these two interpreters, O'Casey wrote for Sally his two greatest women's parts, and Yeats found in her the ideal speaker of his not very dramatic verse. It is difficult to imagine that without Sally and Molly the new theatrical movement could have made the impact it did, first on Dublin and then on London and New York. Fortunately, one does not have to try.

2

They came from a Dublin family on the fringe of the working class. Sally, who was not without an innocent snobbery, loved in her early Abbey years to retail stories of past Allgood greatness, and of a dash of French blood, which certainly looked well in the publicity. Years later, when she was famous, she was invited to spend a weekend with some real county Allgoods in the north of England, and learned that the family had originally come from Devon and that the French blood was a myth. The grandfather, Edward, had been an Army officer posted to Ireland, who settled there and lost caste socially by intermarriage with the natives. His son George repeated the process, becoming a printing compositor and courting pretty Margaret Harold at her parents' junk shop on the Liffey quays. Her Catholic parents opposed her marriage to a Protestant, and the lover would leave notes for her in the drawers of the second-hand furniture standing outside the shop.

Love triumphed, and the Harolds' objection proved to have been perfectly justified. George Allgood made their daughter a dour, narrow, bigotedly Protestant husband. He gave her eight children, four boys and four girls, and insisted that they should be brought up in his faith. She countered his tyranny by guile, and smuggled them to Mass and Confession while he was out at work.

They were a spirited and fun-loving band, with a passion for singing, dancing and reciting, and this too had to be indulged in behind his back; if he came home and caught them at it he would growl: "Stop that music-hall stuff." He was a good craftsman, father of the chapel at his printing works, and a respected member of his Orange lodge. Altogether, an able and probably a frustrated man; and if it was from the wholly Irish mother that the girls had their charm and fascination, the unattractive, partly-English father passed on to them the qualities of doggedness and perseverance which enabled them to become professionals when so many of their contemporaries remained incurably amateur.

George Allgood's death when the youngest child was still a baby in arms left the family poorer but gayer. Mrs. Allgood went back to work in the furniture trade, and her mother— the indomitable grandmother on whom the girls were to model their studies of old women—took charge of the brood. Sally was apprenticed to an upholstery firm, and well-wishers in the Orange lodge found Molly a place in a Protestant orphanage, from which she presently ran away.

The eldest daughter married early and left home, and the family leadership devolved upon Sally (born October 31st, 1883) and her brother Harold, driving the next pair, Molly (born January 12th, 1887) and George, into a defensive alliance and a fierce determination not to be patronised. The strong ties of blood which bound them all were diversified by a great many surface explosions, and this pattern of conduct persisted throughout their lives.

They were a household of young Nationalists. Sally joined Inghinidhe na hEireann a year or two after its foundation by Maud Gonne, and the boys were early members of Griffith's Sinn Fein. The Daughters of Erin paid, as has been shown, particular attention to the dramatic side of their movement, and William Fay was acting as their coach in addition to running his Irish National Theatre Society, the group which (merging with Yeats's and Lady Gregory's Irish Literary Theatre) eventually developed into the Abbey. Willie Fay recognised the quality of the new recruit, and her natural contralto voice, ideal for folk-song and ballad. He enrolled her in the Society, aglow from its triumph with *Kathleen ni Houlihan*, but still rehearsing in the cramped quarters behind a butcher's shop in Camden Street, and giving its occasional performances in the modest Molesworth Hall.

Sally "walked on" in Lady Gregory's first play, *Twenty-Five*, then was given a small speaking part, the Princess Buan, in Yeats's *The King's Threshold*. Padraic Colum recalls her reading it; they were all struck by her resonant voice and the dignity that invested her rather dumpy figure the moment she got upon the stage. "Who is she?" he asked, and was told, "Oh, somebody out of Inini." Yeats turned to Fay and said: "You have an actress there."

3

Their glorious speaking voices are the Allgood attribute people mention first, but the blunt fact is, both girls had ugly Dublin accents till Frank Fay took them in hand. Frank, Willie's elder brother, was the company's elocution coach, and Sally never ceased to acknowledge the magnitude of her debt to him. She must have learned fast, for *The King's Threshold* was produced at the Molesworth Hall on October

8th, 1903, and her speaking of her part gave satisfaction. But she continued to work at vocal exercises. Even in her "Juno" days, Lennox Robinson describes her arriving regularly an hour before rehearsal, and practising "throwing" her voice to the back of the empty house. The remotest seat in the largest theatre never needed to complain of finding Sara Allgood inaudible.

She first created a Synge part when *Riders to the Sea* was put on at the Molesworth Hall on December 3rd, with Honor Lavelle playing old Maurya. And in the new year she had a fresh interest—creeping out from the upholstery shop in her lunch hour, and going down to Lower Abbey Street to watch the workmen convert the old Mechanics' Institute into the little playhouse which was being given to the company by Yeats's wealthy English friend, Miss Horniman. She would lurk timidly behind a pillar, prepared, if challenged, to say she had a message to deliver; but her dream was of the day when she would reign as leading lady on that stage.

What with delays over the conversion and over securing the patent for the theatre, its doors did not open till December 27th, 1904. Yeats had a new verse-play for the occasion, Lady Gregory a new one-act comedy; and it was as Mrs. Fallon of *Spreading the News* that Sally had her first big success. "Till the performance and the applause," she says, "I had no idea that I had got anything but a little part like those I had played before." Mrs. Fallon is not exactly a "great" part either, but it is sharply individualised and very funny, and Sally's previous appearances had been in poetic tragedy. Her comic gift now came as a revelation. Yeats wrote long afterwards: "It is impossible for those of us who are connected with the Abbey management to forget that night in December 1904, when for the first time she rushed among the crowd in *Spreading the News* calling 'Give me back my man!'"

She created Molly Byrne in Synge's next play, *The Well*

of the Saints, in February of 1905—a part in fact much better suited to young Molly, who "walked on" for the first time in the crowd. But the centre of the stage was still held by founder-members of the Society: Honor Lavelle, Maud Gonne's friend Maire Quinn, and Maire nic Shiubhlaigh (Mary Walker), the official leading lady.

Maire nic Shiubhlaigh was beautiful where Sally was merely comely; she had talent, devotion, intense nationalism; her Kathleen ni Houlihan was closely modelled on that of Maud Gonne. Her Nora in *Shadow of the Glen* was moving and sensitive, and had made a particular impression when the company paid its first visit to London. All she lacked was that indefinable gift of personality which was to make Sara Allgood great. Synge himself confirms this when he writes to Frank Fay of her Nora, reputedly her best part: "Miss Walker is clever and charming in the part, but your brother is so strong he dominates the play—unconsciously and inevitably—and of course the woman should dominate."

There now occurred a development which, from Sally's point of view, was exceedingly fortunate. All the members of the Irish National Theatre Society were equal, and amateur in the sense of being unpaid; they acted on the evenings of Thursday, Friday and Saturday each week, and earned their livings at various trades by day. But at the instigation of Miss Horniman, who wished to see them devote more time to the work of her beloved Yeats, it was proposed to turn the Society into a limited liability company, with the three principal playwrights, Yeats, Synge and Lady Gregory, as directors. Miss Horniman offered to guarantee salaries to Willie Fay as producer and to the leading players, so that they could become wholetime professionals.

Sally of course jumped at the chance to put the chair-covering behind her, but the founder-members, headed by Mary Walker and Maire Quinn, resented a plan which, as they saw it, would give them the status of paid servants in what had been their own organisation. They resigned in a body, though agreeing to stay on into December of 1905 in order to see Lady Gregory's full-length play *The White Cockade* through.

That is the official version of the incident, and no doubt accurate enough in general outline. But letters from Mary Walker which have survived among Lady Gregory's papers suggest that she was very loth to go, and that a quite small concession—say, the inclusion of the Fays among the directors—would have persuaded her and her friends to change their minds. If she bowed herself out, it was not without a good deal of pushing on Sally's part, a process in which Lady Gregory appears to have acquiesced.

This was a testing moment for Lady Gregory, who must by now have realised that in Sara Allgood they had a great interpreter, once Mary Walker was out of the way. Would she behave with the consideration of a lady, or with the ruth-lessness of an impresario? Rightly, she chose the impresario's part, and little Miss Walker was out-manœuvred. The sece-ders formed their own company, and later on Maire ni Shiubhlaigh returned to the Abbey in secondary parts, and went with them on their first American tour. But it is hardly surprising that when she came to write her memoirs, Lady Gregory did not figure in a very sympathetic light.

Fay was left with only four trained actors. He had hastily to recruit fresh blood, promote the bit-players (Molly among them) and give the new leading lady all the scope she would take. Sally was triumphant. Kathleen, Maurya, Dectora in *The Shadowy Waters*—all were hers. It did not matter that the first two were crones and that she was still only twenty-three; she would put on one of the Abbey's crushingly heavy grey wigs, copy her grandmother's mannerisms and be a crone to the life. It meant an enormous amount of concentrated work, but of that she was never afraid.

"Synge seems pleased with the rehearsals of *Riders to the Sea*," wrote Frank Fay to Lady Gregory in January of 1906.

"I am too continually teaching Miss Allgood to know if she is good; but Wright watched last Friday night's rehearsal and says she grips in the part. Her sister (Molly, a very determined young lady) promises to make something and I am taking her in hand. She is as careful about things as if her bread and butter depended on her doing what I show her right."

In the summer, Miss Horniman took the company on tour to England and Scotland, and he again reported to Lady Gregory: "Miss Allgood is doing wonderful work. She is the only one in the crowd who is able to hold the stage against my brother or myself . . . she grips every audience in Kathleen and in Mrs. Fallon."

Kathleen ni Houlihan in Yeats's (or more accurately, Yeats's and Lady Gregory's) political one-acter was, wrote Sally, "the part I had wanted for years. There had been many Kathleens; everyone had played it their own way. Miss Maud Gonne's performance, the original Kathleen, I couldn't clearly remember as I was very young at the time." Other players had stressed the supernatural element, but "I had a different conception . . . I call into my thoughts all those who have died for Ireland. I say to myself, their deaths were victory. Ireland too will be victorious. I fill myself with joy. Dervorgilla, that is the sorrow of Ireland. But Kathleen looks into the future."

The actress who had the honour to play Kathleen personified Ireland. For many in the first generation of Abbey playgoers, the supreme experience was to hear Sara Allgood's velvet voice speaking the great final lines, *They shall be remembered for ever*. . . . The centre of the stage was now hers by right of talent, and there was small sign of a rival sufficiently well endowed to push her off again.

Except, of course, for Molly.

4

Molly, after the orphanage episode, had been apprenticed to a dressmaker, then had worked in a shop, but she was as much resolved as Sally to make herself an actress, and equally, not to do it under Sally's patronage or shadow. She found herself another name, turning her "Mary" into Irish and taking the "O'Neill" from an aunt (of whom nothing is remembered save that the girls as children had been forced to brush her long hair). As Maire O'Neill she played in crowd scenes in 1905, being chaperoned to rehearsals by her grandmother. She was eighteen, which is not so very child-ish, and it had never been considered necessary to chaperone Sally. But this was doubtless the family's way of recognising that Molly was a handful.

Perhaps she was not strictly beautiful, with her tip-tilted nose and the "little bulldog chin" on which her lover was to comment. (Sally had this Allgood chin too, but more pronouncedly.) But Molly's was the heartbreaking prettiness which can be so much more dangerous than classical beauty. The big dark eyes set in the delicate heart-shaped face could flash fire or melt to tenderness; the rare shy smile was des-cribed by one enraptured critic as "witch-like in its roguery". Above all, she had the combination of virginal Irish in-nocence and strong come-hither so well calculated to drive men mad. She attracted as a woman, and then eluded as a child. (She was in fact physically a late developer, and this involved her in difficulties over which, she told her daughter long afterwards, Synge was invariably patient and kind.)

By temperament she was a rebel, unwilling to submit to

any discipline except that which was self-imposed. She would work like a demon to make herself a better actress, but for literature and culture as such, or for the social position and acceptance which meant so much to Sally, she did not give a damn. Her younger brother George was her chief ally against family authority, and the person she loved best in the world.

This was the fatally fascinating creature who was to inspire and devastate the last three years of John Millington Synge.

The Walker secession cleared Molly's way as well as Sally's, put her on the payroll, and brought her two Synge roles: first the small one of Cathleen in *Riders*, and then, as his interest in her increased, the leading one of Nora in *Shadow of the Glen*. This was not a development pleasing to Sally, who had expected to inherit all Maire nic Shiubhlaigh's parts. But she was not competing against an unworldly political idealist now. Her rival was another Allgood, with a streak of ruthlessness to match her own.

Power was being concentrated in fewer hands at the Abbey, and the wise actress found herself a protector. Yeats was too Olympian and remote, and Willie Fay was preoccupied with the other beauty of the company, Brigit O'Dempsey, whom he was presently to marry. Sally secured the perfect complement and ally in Lady Gregory. Human motives are always mixed, and I am not suggesting that she failed to appreciate Lady Gregory's greatness, either as a person or as a playwright. But she also knew on which side her bread was—however thinly at this period—buttered.*

---

* The thinness of the butter in the Abbey's first decade is demonstrated in contracts signed by Sally and Molly, and preserved among Lady Gregory's papers. Sally's reads:

"Agreement made this 14th day of February 1908 between The National Theatre Society Ltd. of the one part and Sara Allgood of the other part. Whereby it is agreed that in consideration of the sum of £2-0-0 paid weekly by the said National Theatre Society Ltd. to the said Sara Allgood, the said Sara Allgood agrees to rehearse and perform to the best of her skill and ability such parts as she may be cast for in plays

Her letters to Lady Gregory are those of a flatterer, and the
element of gush in them increases with the years.

But young Molly, in acquiring or being acquired by
Synge, might be thought to have done better than anyone,
since he was not only the company's most gifted dramatist,
but the Director permanently resident in Dublin, and the
one who accompanied the players on their English and
Scottish tours.

There were two tours in that summer of 1906; unfortunately Miss Horniman also travelled with them, and thus
observed at first hand how little discipline Mr. Synge
troubled to impose. Molly was soon in her bad books for
"rowdiness", though none of the girls seemed to her to
behave with proper decorum. By the end of the second
tour, she thought she detected a falling-off in J.M.'s attentions to the younger Allgood. "Of course Mr. Synge is
willing to give her up now; three months of one girl on his
knee doubtless leads him to wish for a change."

Yeats and Lady Gregory certainly wished for it. It seemed
to them disastrous that Synge at thirty-four, and just
beginning to reap the fame his genius deserved, should

performed by the Society and carry out such other duties as she may be
called on to perform. It is also agreed that the said salary shall be inclusive
of seven performances weekly if required. This engagement to commence
on February 14th, 1908 at the Abbey Theatre, and continue in force one
month's notice on either side.

"That should the said Sara Allgood be imperfect (provided a reasonable
time has been allowed for rehearsals) and not speak the Author's lines at
any performance she shall be subject to suspension and have no claim for
salary beyond the proportion due up to such imperfect performance till
decision of the Directors on the matter shall be given.

"That should the said Sara Allgood conduct herself in or out of the
Theatre in a manner calculated to bring discredit upon the Society she
shall be liable to instant dismissal and have no claim or salary whatever.

"That the said Sara Allgood shall conform to all rules of the Society."

Molly's contract was identical except that her salary was £1-5-0
weekly.

The clause referring to conduct in or out of the Theatre was no idle
threat. Miss Horniman tried to make the Directors dismiss actresses
under it, merely for "talking to strange men" out of a railway carriage
window during an English tour. Such behaviour, she wrote to Lady
Gregory, was "bad enough for a jury".

entangle himself permanently with a chit of nineteen, a Roman Catholic, and his equal neither by birth nor by education. Sally sided with them. Here again her motives were probably mixed, and she could certainly remember, in her own parents, the unhappy consequences of a marriage between people of incompatible temperaments and faiths. But to Molly, it looked like a particularly treacherous form of sucking-up. She left home and went to stay with the married sister, rather than remain under the same roof with Sally; and at the theatre, the two young leading ladies were not on speaking terms.

It was awkward for everyone. Synge did what he could, urging his beloved to make it up with her sister: "you know I've a great respect for her in many ways." Lady Gregory would surely have done better to address herself to her own favourite, but once again Molly appears to have had the benefit of an outsider's advice. "When Sally went," Lady Gregory notes in her journal, "I told Molly that my sister Mrs. Waithman and I used to have quarrels until our mother insisted on our kissing each other afterwards, and we disliked that so much that we gave up quarrelling. If it goes on I think I must supervise a reconciliation."

She had reason to be anxious, for the two girls had what amounted to a long duet in her first, and probably her finest, one-act tragedy, *The Gaol Gate*, which was due to have its production when the autumn season opened. But the first night on October 20th revealed that astonishing Allgood faculty, noted by colleagues throughout the years, of being temperamental and tiresome up to the very last minute, and then sinking themselves utterly in their parts as soon as the curtain rose.

Sally's experience as Kathleen and as Maurya already fitted her to play the heroic mother, who glories that her son has died rather than betray his friends. But Molly, with barely six months' training, must have been stretched to the uttermost to convey the anguish of the young wife who will never again hold her warm comrade in her arms. Her grief when she learns of his execution is expressed in a long poetic chant, and it is hard to credit that Molly, in this first attempt at one of her finest parts, could have attained the full poignancy remembered by playgoers who saw her do it later in her career. But she must have given a remarkable performance, for the critics went out of their way to praise "Miss O'Neill's singing of the Caoine".

And a better reconciler than Lady Gregory was on the way, in the shape of a rival from London. Miss Horniman, who had given the company its theatre primarily for the production of Yeats's poetic plays, was dissatisfied with their lack of popular success; and Yeats himself had declared that Catholic Ireland could never produce an actress able to convey sensual passion, though quite what sensual passion there was to be conveyed in the plays he had written up to that period, I do not know.

At all events, a distinguished actress with the stage name of Miss Darragh, a friend of Miss Horniman, was brought in to create the name-part in his new version of the Deirdre legend, and stayed on to play Maire nic Shiubhlaigh's part of Dectora in the revised version of his *Shadowy Waters*. She was Irish by birth but English by training, and appears to have been personally a nice woman, who used her influence with Miss Horniman to try to make things easier for the much harassed Willie Fay. No doubt she was a competent performer in the rather stilted tradition of Edwardian stage-ladyhood, but its incompatibility with the Abbey style was laughable; as Willie Fay said, it was like putting a Rolls-Royce to run with a herd of mountain ponies.

Sally and Molly played the Musicians who act as Chorus to the work, and Sally further won Yeats's regard by composing the music for the final dirge, "They are gone, they are gone . . ." Yeats had his own ideas on stage music (as, indeed, on every other aspect of production);* it should, he explained in the preface to *Deirdre*, "be associated with words that must never lose the intonation of passionate speech. No vowel must ever be prolonged unnaturally, no word of mine must ever change into a mere musical note, no singer of my words must ever cease to be a man and become an instrument. . . . It is very difficult for a musician who is not a speaker to do exactly what I want." In Miss Allgood he had found the happy exception, and he considered that she had got "the full association of speech" into the dirge.

Dublin's reception of *Deirdre* was lukewarm, and it was patent to Miss Darragh herself that she was a failure. She returned to London early in 1907, and Sally took over both her parts when next the plays were revived. Nothing more was heard from Yeats about her inability to convey sensual passion. Henceforth he was her staunchest supporter, and only regretted that none of them, as dramatists, had yet been able to give her full scope.

He was always more reserved about Molly. He called her "lyrical, sophisticated and subtle", but held that she could not achieve real tragedy, only pathos, and that she did not think enough. In this last criticism he was probably quite justified, but to call her sophisticated is palpably absurd.

Sally could hold an audience by the splendour of her verse delivery and the increasing majesty of her presence, but Molly was a wholly instinctive actress, who had to feel an earthy reality in every part, or she became colourless. Thus she could interpret Synge's heroines, because for all the rainbow beauty of their language they have their feet very firmly on the ground. But it was not in her to come anywhere near the cerebral and disembodied spirits of Yeats.

* Yeats's idea of how his verse should be spoken, crystal-clear to himself, was notoriously difficult to convey to the performers. From Maureen Delany I had a pleasant story of Yeats rehearsing Arthur Sinclair in a soliloquy, and booming his satisfaction: "Mr. Sinclair, you've got it—you've got it!" Puzzled but gratified, Sinclair did his best at the next rehearsal to repeat his rendering exactly, only to be greeted this time by sepulchral gloom: "Mr. Sinclair, you've lost it—you've lost it!"

5

Those of us over whom the work and personality of Synge have cast a spell almost as potent as that exercised by Keats were in the habit of speculating about his love-letters to Molly Allgood, the girl who more than any other inspired Pegeen Mike of *The Playboy of the Western World*, and then created her on the stage. Might they not, we hoped, prove as rich and gay and delicate as the love-making in the play itself? With the publication of Professor David H. Greene and Edward M. Stephens's monumental life of Synge in 1959 the contents of a good many of them were revealed, and our disappointment was correspondingly severe.

This good man and great writer, who understood human nature and particularly the feminine heart so well, commits in the supreme crisis of his emotional life the elementary errors against which any advice-to-the-lovelorn column could have warned him. He harps continually on the points which would be better left unstressed, the difference in their ages, his own delicate health, the fact that he has staked all on a last love, the fatal consequences to him if it should fail; it is almost as though he were challenging her to destroy the hope on which his existence depends.

He scolds and lectures, wants her to read more, improve her mind, become "the best-educated actress in Europe", wear quieter clothes, not laugh so loud, behave like a lady and win her way into his mother's good graces. He is imprudently and naggingly jealous of the boys near her own age with whom she flirts, particularly one Dossie Wright, the company's personable young electrician and bit-part player. It is the behaviour of an amorous dotard in a comedy by

Molière*—or, one might pay him the compliment of saying, a tragi-comedy by Synge.

Certainly he was not robust, but there is no reason to suppose than in 1906 the cancer which was to kill him had declared itself. And he was at the height of his powers; the hand that wrote those unfortunate letters was also drawing the Playboy and Pegeen. To say that Molly *was* Pegeen is, of course, to over-simplify. The idea of the play had been in his mind before he met her, and he had already found elements of the character—its wildness, its alternations of tenderness and ferocity, its cruel streak—in girls on the Aran and Blasket islands. He was attracted to Molly because she was that kind of girl; but instead of being a peasant, she was lower-middle-class Dublin, and therefore (if she would only take a little more trouble with her self-improvement) within his reach.

And yet he knew Pegeen so well! He knew that what she wanted was a hero; not in order to be dominated—there is nothing in Pegeen of the dreary little masochists who pass for heroines on our contemporary stage—but because a hero could open the door for her into a fuller and richer life. What chance would Christy have had with Pegeen if he had passed the two days in her father's public house complaining about her manners and his own ill-health?

The depressing truth was, that in his personal life Synge had been too long the cossetted Irish mother's-boy. His mother could not understand or sympathise with his work, but she loved him dearly and her love was returned. It had become second nature with him to pour complaints into a female ear; it is pathetic to see him trying to check himself, and failing. He was also in awe of his mother, and had been virtually engaged for a year before he summoned the courage to tell her. He was living with her in her suburban villa,

* Molière was in much the same position *vis-à-vis* Armande Béjart, who has come down to us as a wholly unsympathetic character through her treatment of her great lover, but who may, equally with Molly, have had some justification on her side.

Glendalough House, Glenageary, and he did not bring
Molly home.

They met at Bray, or some other railway station, and spent
their Sundays walking by the sea or over the hills. And when
they could keep from quarrelling, these were days of ecstatic
happiness to him, but it is doubtful if she enjoyed them so
much. She had been on her feet all week in the gruelling
rehearsals and performances of a small and overworked
repertory company. She was not really a child of nature,
though to him she might symbolise the iridescent beauty of
the Wicklow Hills. She was a city sparrow, and she much
preferred to find herself in a cheerful crowd.

"If you begin hankering after commonplace pleasures
and riches and that sort of thing we shall both be made
wretched," he warned her. Riches meant, in fact, very little to
her, though they ran through her fingers when she had them.
But if by commonplace pleasures he meant going on seaside
excursions with the rest of the company, flirting with
several boys at once and walking home arm in arm with
Dossie Wright, the blunt truth was that she not only hankered
but intended to go on participating. It was a young girl's
natural relaxation after a week of strain and toil, and it took
her into a sunny, carefree world where for all his towering
imagination he could not follow her.

Perhaps it is unfair to judge him on his letters; perhaps he
sometimes found Christy's "poet's talking and bravery of
heart" to woo her with. Certainly, through the kindness of
her daughter, I have seen more lover-like letters than seem
to have fallen into Professor Greene's net. One written as
his work on *Playboy* neared completion, which shows the
depth and also the dreadful vulnerability of his feeling for
her, ends:

I send some lines I scratched off last night, if they make
you smile remember they are a first draft only. I send also
a foolish letter I wrote last night. Now for the Play Boy—
God confound him!

The "lines" may have been one of four unpublished poems
found among Molly's papers. The first enumerates her Synge
parts to that date:

> To you Bride, Nora, Kathleen, Molly Byrne,
> I of my age have brought the pride and power,
> And seen my hardness in your sweetness turn
> A new delight for our long fame a dower.
>
> And now you bring to me your young girl's pride,
> And sweeten with your sweetness all my days,
> Telling me dreams where our red lips have cried
> The long low cry that folds all earthly praise.
>
> And so in all our lot we hold a mart
> Of your young joy and my too gloomy art.

Two commemorate happy moments:

> The grass and celandine,
> The blackbird and the bee,
> The birches topped with green
> Have met my love and me.
>
> We've met the lark and wren,
> The cowslip and the rose,
> The furse that's in the glen,
> The flies are on the sloes.
>
> We've kissed our fingers tips,
> Our ears, and double chin,
> Our red and happy lips,
> Among our kith and kin,
> All things abroad today,
> To play the Masque of May.
>
>
> With one long kiss
> Were you near by,
> You'd break the dismal cloud that is
> On all my sky.

With one long kiss
If you were near
You'd sweeten days I take amiss
When lonely here.

With one long kiss
You'd make for me
A golden paradise of this
Day's beggary.

And the last crystallises a more characteristic mood of
despair:

I brought you where the stars and moon of night
Filled earth and air with dreams of strange delight.
I taught you notes of blackbirds, wrens and larks,
And showed you ruddy buds with curious marks.
I made you listen to far wings of rooks,
And held you in my arms in mossy nooks
And then I thought my long long waiting done
As sick men watch the rising of an autumn sun.

And then I saw you go your own sure way
To oily men made rich with cheap display.
So I go lonely to the lonely hills
Where still the fragrant air my breathing fills,
And I lie low with many a deadly weed
And write a heavy curse to fill my creed
And cry for some hot brand to sear my lips
Which my wild madness laid upon your finger tips.

Was she at all in love with him? I find it very hard to
credit. Her letters to him have not survived—no one thinks
to keep the love-letters of the Fanny Brawnes and the Molly
Allgoods—but it is plain from his that quarrels were con-
tinuous. He speaks in anguish of her stony face, her looks
of hard contempt. And when he had irritated her beyond
bearing, she would scribble her reaction across his letters:
"idiotic", or "appalling", or "I don't care if I never see you
again". Yet something kept her faithful, at any rate to the

extent of not actually throwing him over, for three years.

A combination of factors, perhaps. First there was his genius; in his possession of that he was truly a hero, and Molly in her untutored way was always better able to appreciate people's qualities than the more socially ambitious Sally. She knew that Synge was a great man, she felt the enormous flattery of his condescending to her, he of whom even Yeats and Lady Gregory would speak with something like awe. To dominate so gifted and powerful a creature was an experience few nineteen-year-olds could have resisted.

And a very strong reinforcement must have been the amount of opposition her engagement to him aroused. Nobody wanted it, neither his family, nor her family, nor the Olympian figures who ruled at the theatre. If she broke with Synge, it would give them all undisguised satisfaction, and to one of Molly's temperament, that would be reason good for hanging on.

Lastly, in June of 1907, there was the balm of a shared success.

6

It certainly did not feel like a success, when at the end of January *The Playboy of the Western World* was put on at the Abbey, and howled down for a week. It was virtually impossible to judge either play or performance, though Synge wrote to Molly in the middle of the week: "You don't know how much I admired the way you are playing P. Mike in spite of all the row."

The riots over, the company went back to their internal troubles—Miss Horniman had insisted on bringing in an English producer for the Yeats plays, and Willie Fay's position was growing every week more difficult—and Synge, who had obtained his mother's reluctant consent to his marriage, went ahead with his modest plans. "I counted up my money last night, and if all goes well I think we shall have £150 for our first year, if we get married soon, that is £3 a week."

Molly's salary was £1-5-0 a week, and Sally's £2; yet Sally, one is amused to note, had her photograph on the cover of the programme for the big English and Scottish tour which began in May. The theatre's founders had set their faces against any form of starring, and the home programmes were chastely decorated with the figures of Cuchulain and his hound, as they are to this day. But when it came to an overseas tour, there was really no point in concealing the fact that Miss Sara Allgood was by now a draw.

The Directors funked presenting *Playboy* anywhere but in Oxford and London; but its reception there was enough to establish both Synge's and Molly's fame. The play was recognised as an original and fascinating masterpiece, and the big personal triumph went to the Pegeen Mike. It is generally agreed that Willie Fay, the first Christy, was not young or glamorous enough for the part, and Sally found Widow Quin "a part scarcely to my liking" (in which she shows her limitation, for a first-rate Widow can act a second-rate Pegeen off the stage, as Molly herself was to prove in later years).

They all came home triumphant, and Synge and Molly had what was perhaps their one really happy holiday, staying —for propriety's sake in separate cottages—in the Wicklow hills. They planned their future, their little flat in a part of Dublin well away from everybody's relations, and his next play, which was to be yet another version of the Deirdre story (Yeats and A. E. had already tried their hands at it, *il fallait passer par là*), and which might perhaps give her an even more wonderful part than Pegeen. Synge decided to set his health in order by undergoing a recommended gland operation in September, and when the surgeons operated, they found a malignant growth and knew that he was doomed. But they did not tell him, and nor, of course, did Molly know.

The October season opened well, with fine parts for Sally in Fitzmaurice's *The Country Dressmaker* and in Lady Gregory's one-act *Dervorgilla*, which shows the noble and elegiac old age of the Irish Helen, the woman whose faithlessness brought the English into Ireland.

Synge to Molly, Glendalough House, November 15th, 1907:

Dearest Love,

How are you today? I was tired after all the compliments, but I am as usual now. About tomorrow; if it is wet come by the quarter to two or the quarter to three, as you find it most convenient, and if it is fine come by the quarter to three, so that I'll have time for a little walk, that will leave us three hours together. Of course I depend on you not to come at all if you are not well enough. I was too busy with Deirdre to write to you this morning so—as you can see—this is an after-dinner note. I wonder which of my letters it is that you like so much. You mustn't mind my letters being a little dry these times, because I am pouring out my heart to you in Deirdre the whole day long.

I am pleased with it now, but that doesn't mean much as I go backward and forward in my feelings to my work every second day—at least when they are in this stage. I am half inclined to write to old Yeats and ask him straight out to sell me your picture.* Would that be a good plan? If it goes to the Abbey we'll see no more of it.

Now do take all possible care of yourself my own treasure of the world.

            Your old Tramp.

But the actual administration of the theatre was going through worsening troubles. The English producer had been

* Presumably her portrait by Sarah Purser, which was to hang in the Abbey green-room.

frozen out, Miss Horniman in disgust had transferred her interest and most of her money to the founding of what became
the Gaiety Theatre in Manchester, and Willie Fay had found
his authority seriously weakened by the period of dual control. It is sad but not surprising to record that Molly was the
principal culprit, and he complained of her conduct in bitter
letters to Lady Gregory:

Dec. 1st, 1907. ". . . Mac* and Molly are the worst offenders,
and I'll not put up with her insolence and insubordination
for it makes my position impossible if youngsters like her and
Mac can defy my authority. Molly was exceedingly difficult
to manage on the summer tour and uses her intimacy with
Mr. Synge to do as she likes."

Dec. 17th. ". . . I wrote yesterday to Mr. Yeats with
reference to lack of punctuality in attending rehearsal and
called his attention to the fact that out of seven rehearsals on
tour, Molly Allgood was late for all but one, and on one
occasion was an hour late, in Edinburgh."

His proposed remedy was, that the company's right to
appeal to the Directors over his head should cease, and that
hire-and-fire authority should be vested in himself. Alas,
"the dog it was that died". By one stroke he had set against
him actors and Directors too. Synge would not sacrifice Molly
to any producer, however justly outraged; and Yeats and
Lady Gregory, though they had stood by Willie Fay staunchly
till that moment, would not relinquish full powers in the
theatre which they regarded as their creation, though in
truth it was a Fay creation too. They were not, they told him,
disposed to make any changes. The Fay brothers and Brigit
O'Dempsey resigned.

And once again the theatre proved its resilience; it went
on without them, as it had done after the Walker defection.
Arthur Sinclair stepped into some of Willie's parts, and a new

* Arthur Sinclair, whose real name was Francis Quinton MacDonnell.
When he joined the company as a part-timer in 1904 he was a junior
clerk in a solicitor's office, and took a stage name to conceal the fact of
his play-acting from his employers.

discovery, Fred O'Donovan, brought the necessary good looks and dash to others, like the Playboy. Dramatists like Norreys Connell and Lady Gregory, actors including Sally tried their hands at production; though they were very glad to hand over to Lennox Robinson when he appeared on the scene two years later.

But Molly had now to meet a more implacable enemy than Willie Fay.

7

In April of 1908 Sally was lent to Miss Horniman's new Manchester company to play her first Shakespearean role, Isabella in *Measure for Measure*. The *Manchester Guardian* praised her in this rather thankless part, but found it was not the equal of her Maurya in *Riders to the Sea*, "perhaps the finest piece of tragic acting that any English-speaking actress has done in our time".

As a result of her absence, Molly got the part of the old countrywoman in Lady Gregory's revised version of *The Workhouse Ward*, and proved that the Allgood genius for turning in a trice from youth to age was hers also. Lennox Robinson has described the transformation which would come over her as she stood in the wings waiting for her cue; at one moment a jaunty girl, cigarette in mouth, and then every muscle in her body seemed to alter. In a double bill of *Workhouse Ward* and *Playboy* she completely baffled one of his friends, who left asking "What is she really like?"

Synge had begun to think of a definite date for the wedding. But at the end of this month acute pain in his side sent him into hospital again, and this time an inoperable tumour was found. He was still allowed to hope, and even

seemed for a time to be recovering, but all thought of the
wedding was put aside. Molly, though she had no idea how
serious his condition was, seems to have become kinder and
more patient; his chief complaint now was that when they
were apart she did not write often enough. His mother was
dying, and he himself began to feel death close. His moving
little poem "A Question", written in September, shows
Molly in a new light. For a moment she seems almost capable
of a ferocity of passion like his own.

Driven by pain and restlessness, he went abroad in the
last stages of his mother's illness, returning only for her
funeral in November. The suburban villa was now desolate
indeed, but he struggled on with his *Deirdre*, and when Molly
came out to see him she would act over what he had written;
thus the legend that she "acted Deirdre for him as he lay
dying" arose. But by the time he was actually admitted to
hospital, he was too ill to write any more.

He re-entered hospital for the last time in February of
1909, and died on March 24th. Molly told his nephew
afterwards that when the full truth of his condition came
home to her, she rushed to one priest after another, seeking
to have a mass said for his recovery, and that they refused
because he was a Protestant; after which she gave up, for a
long time, all religious observance herself.

There is no doubt that Synge's death shook her profoundly.
But I suspect that relief at her escape, and remorse at feeling
such relief, made up a good part of her distraction.

"Either he'd have strangled her or she'd have run away
from him at the end of a year," opines the person who knew
her best. Pegeen Mair may be considered prejudiced, but she
seems to me to view her mother's character and career with
an admirably affectionate detachment.

Nevertheless, literature owes a debt of gratitude to Molly
Allgood for the part she played in the life of Synge. She gave
him stimulus, which is much more important than happiness
to an artist, and particularly to one whose time is short.

G

Without her, *Playboy* would not have tingled with the same electric excitement, and *Deirdre* might not have been written at all. *Playboy* is radiant with the triumph of winning her, *Deirdre* poignant with the anguish of losing her. If one may choose an epitaph for the story of Synge's last and greatest love, it shall not be his Deirdre's furious railing against death or Conchubor's bitter realisation of what it means to long for youth in vain. It shall be the more serene acceptance of Lady Gregory's Gormleith, the Queen in *Kincora*, after her siding with his enemies has brought her husband to his end:

> It is not Brian would wish to die the death of a man that is lessening and stiffening, the time he grows attentive to his bed, but of a winner that is merry and shouting, the time his enemies are put down. I was maybe a right wife for him. A right wife, a lucky wife, in spite of all!

8

Molly was given no time for repining; the Abbey grind went on. Synge's tragic and relatively early death meant an enormous increase of interest in his plays. *Playboy* was given almost without opposition in Dublin, and a critic prophesied that "Miss Maire O'Neill will speedily stand upon a footing of equality with her sister." The summer season in London brought them further laurels. Sally was hailed as "the one genuine tragedienne on the English-speaking stage", and all the girls of the company, but particularly Molly, were found to have a Spanish quality. "They use their eyes very much as a Spanish girl does, and Miss O'Neill has something of the Spanish modulation and inflexion of voice."

Even the August holiday was eaten into by rehearsals, for Lady Gregory had secured from Bernard Shaw the first production of *The Shewing-Up of Blanco Posnet*, banned by the English Censor on account of its alleged blasphemy; and she and Yeats had triumphantly worsted an attempt by Dublin Castle to repeat the prohibition in Ireland. This was the play whose production Sally tried and found beyond her powers, and Lady Gregory took it over.

Sally herself played Feemy Evans, a bad piece of miscasting; she needed nobility in a part, and failed, then and in subsequent roles, to suggest the physical characteristics of a harlot. Molly on the other hand had a natural raffishness which enabled her to play harlots with relish. In this play she had the small part of the woman whose baby dies, and was so moving in it that, it is said, she reduced G. B. S. to tears for the first and last time at one of his own plays. More importantly for her own future, she made a profound impression on a young journalist, sent over to report on the play by the *Manchester Guardian*—one George Herbert Mair.

The last tribute the Abbey could pay to Synge was to put on his *Deirdre*, and Yeats and Lady Gregory toiled through the early part of the winter to extract from its many versions a single actable shape. Molly, as the person who had been closest to him while he was writing it, was called in to collaborate. Brought thus directly under Yeats's eye, she seems to have won more approval than in the days when he regarded her as Synge's calamity, and he encouraged her to describe premonitions of her lover's death. She obliged with three, but like most of the occult experiences people were induced to divulge to Yeats, they have a suspiciously Yeatsian flavour.

Lady Gregory was more guarded. She appreciated Molly as an actress but not as a trouble-maker, and she could hardly have forgotten those bitter letters from Willie Fay. It is significant that in describing the work done on *Deirdre* in *Our Irish Theatre*, she makes no mention of Molly's help.

The play was given at the Abbey in January of 1910. Yeats was disappointed in Molly; he said she produced "nothing out of a brooding mind". And when William Archer saw her in London he found that "she seemed to be moving harmoniously through a melancholy monotonous dream. Only on reading did I discover that Mr. Synge had conceived Deirdre as a wilful imperious creature, not without a spice of the devil in her." But other critics declared that she "achieved a wonderful triumph and acted throughout with a weird pathos and rare beauty". It is easy to credit that the play may have been, for her, too haunted by the dying Synge. She certainly possessed the "spice of the devil", but she probably needed to stand further away from the work before she could put it into Deirdre's lines.

But of her Pegeen Mike there could be no question; it grew better and better. Young Mr. Mair, who had again contrived to get himself sent to Dublin, sent back to the *Manchester Guardian* a splendidly evocative picture of an evening at the Abbey, the strong sense of audience participation ("I realised what being in one of the two or three live centres of dramatic art in Europe means"), and a description of *Playboy* in which he found himself "spellbound by the strange and entrancing fascination of Miss Maire O'Neill".

And when the play was repeated in the London summer season, James Douglas wrote in *The Leader* that "Miss O'Neill unconsciously dominates the men she acts with. She has race in her. She holds her head up and walks and uses the gestures of a conquerer. As Pegeen . . . she is swift, protean, a ruler of men, and yet as simple and fresh as a wild strawberry." He ended his review with a plea to make the vitality of the Irish theatre contagious. There should be Welsh, Scottish, Cornish plays, all racy and of the soil. "We must get away from the city pavements to the rural parishes, from Piccadilly to the villages, from the shop windows to the shires." The Abbey players had indeed brought a breath of fresh air into the stuffiness of the English Edwardian stage.

Synge's *Deirdre* was followed at the Abbey by Yeats's, and at last Sally got the part. She had again played second fiddle—that is to say, First Musician—to the Deirdre of Mrs. Patrick Campbell, to whom she had been lent when the play was put on in London late in 1908. She was grateful, however, for that opportunity; Mrs. Pat was kind to her and taught her a good deal, besides impressing on her the importance of sticking to serious drama and not being lured away by lucrative musical-comedy offers. And Mrs. Pat on her side never ceased to praise Sally's combination of warmth with purity; she believed it was a quality which could only be found in an Irish actress.

On the summer tours, Molly now had equal billing with Sally and Arthur Sinclair. The bitter quarrels were a thing of the past, but there were always minor jealousies. Lennox Robinson, who had joined the company as producer, remembered that "there was a certain rivalry between them; there needn't have been. Sally could do things that Molly couldn't touch, and vice versa. Sally's tragedy was grandiose, Molly's intimate and personal." (But in truth Molly was the more versatile; in later years she took over most of Sally's tragic parts in England, Australia and America, and gave them a quite different, more earthy quality, which some playgoers preferred.)

These were great years at the Abbey, despite the continual financial anxiety. Synge had become a classic, Yeats and Lady Gregory were still producing important work, and a new generation of young playwrights, the so-called "Cork realists", arrived with lower-middle-class dramas containing fat acting parts, so that there was always something fresh to take to London in the summer.

T. C. Murray, one of the "realists", records that "the Abbey season had indeed become almost a fashionable cult. If you wished to be considered a person of fine taste, you patronised the Royal Court Theatre in Sloane Square." (Liverpool, Manchester, Oxford and Cambridge were the other towns usually toured.) One of Murray's plays, *Maurice Harte*, actually had its first night at the Royal Court and not at the Abbey. Sally played the domineering mother, entirely to the dramatist's satisfaction. "On that night, Sara Allgood's study of the character seemed inspired . . . maternal love, pride, ambition, anger, despair, all the gamut in a woman's emotional make-up was laid bare."

Dublin was proud of its two leading ladies; the flower sellers in O'Connell Street gave them a buttonhole every evening as they went to the theatre, and would never take a penny in return. But still the plays were not supported with sufficient regularity to ensure decent salaries. Tempting London offers were refused, though Lady Gregory was unhappily aware that they would not be refused for ever. In the autumn of 1910 it was Molly's turn to be lent to the Gaiety for an English tour, playing Candida, and Synge's Nora. She was billed as "the wonderful Irish actress", and audiences were reminded that only her loyalty to Ireland had kept her at the Abbey.

This was the tour from which, according to Lennox Robinson, she vowed she would return with three engagement rings—and kept her word. Synge was, if not forgotten, at any rate conveniently transmuted. He had become "my J.M.", an enhancement of her prestige and of her ability to get her own way. If Synge in spirit still haunted the Abbey, he must often have worn a wry smile.*

But one at least of the engagement rings fitted. It was from G. H. Mair, the young *Manchester Guardian* critic whom she had so bewitched by her Pegeen. In June of 1911 she married him, and the company found itself without a Pegeen for that important landmark, its first American tour.

* Perhaps he did haunt it. Maureen Delany, who joined the company in 1916 and was too young to have seen Synge in the flesh, told me that once while waiting for her cue she saw a very dark man, in vaguely old-fashioned clothes, standing in the wings on the opposite side of the stage. He was watching the play with intense concentration, and a moment later had disappeared. She was entirely convinced that she had seen Synge.

Another actress, Eithne Magee, was recruited, and Lady Gregory, who was in charge of the tour, rehearsed her as they went along. The play provoked riots as alarming as the Dublin ones, and the company weathered them gallantly, but Sally never forgot this stormy first reception in the country that was eventually to become her own. "I don't feel I can bear another *Playboy* riot," she told Lady Gregory years afterwards, when hesitating over an American tour of O'Casey plays. But if she found herself sometimes shouted down as Widow Quin, she gripped American audiences utterly as Kathleen, as Maurya, and as the bereaved mother of *Gaol Gate*.

The experiences of the tour cemented her friendship with Lady Gregory, and alone among the players, she became a regular visitor to Coole. The friendship did a great deal for her, both professionally and socially. She learnt that "Lady Augusta Gregory" was not the correct way to address a letter to her hostess, and a *grande dame* manner was added to her natural warmth—not always to the satisfaction of her colleagues. Here there are two opinions about Sally. Those whom she befriended adored her, but young girls in the company, and most of the amateurs who came in to do bit parts, were apt to find themselves brushed contemptuously aside. It is generally agreed that of the two, naughty wilful Molly was the kinder and more helpful to a beginner.

But Sally needed more money. Not only was she a better business woman than Molly, but she now saw her sister prosperously married, and returning between confinements to well-paid work on the English stage. Moreover, the main burden of supporting their mother fell upon Sally, and the Abbey's finances, which seemed to have found their solution in American touring, again became precarious when the outbreak of war caused audiences to shrink.

In 1914 Sally left for a spell in repertory at Liverpool. That, Lady Gregory could perhaps regard as a necessary

extension of her experience. But it must have appeared a sad
fall from grace when in 1915 she undertook to portray win-
some Irish girlhood at loggerheads with the English upper
classes in Mr. J. Hartley Manners's comedy *Peg O' My Heart*.
"The one genuine tragedienne on the English-speaking
stage" seemed to have turned her back on greatness.

It was likewise ironic that she who in her early twenties
had played so many old women should now at thirty-three
impersonate a romping teenager. Photographs of her in the
part give a painful impression of mutton dressed as lamb.
But the photographs of another era are notoriously misleading, and audiences everywhere, seeking an escape from
the grim realities of war, found it in Sara Allgood's Peg.
Perhaps Sally herself did too, for in this year her two eldest
brothers were killed; they had joined the British armed forces
in spite of the Sinn Fein past.

She was invited by the J. and N. Tait management to lead
a tour of Australia and New Zealand with the all-conquering
Peg. They sailed early in 1916, and the leading man was a
handsome boy called Gerald Henson.

9

Given that the popular art of one generation does tend to
look silly to the next, still it is almost incomprehensible that
our fathers could have been ravished by a play so weirdly
amateurish and inept as Mr. J. Hartley Manners's *Peg O'
My Heart*. The explanation must be that the part of staunch,
merry, father-fixated Irish-American Peg, though it would
never have got past the dialect experts at the Abbey, did give
scope to the charm of two actresses, Laurette Taylor, who

created it in America and then in London (the author
receiving the recompense of her hand in marriage), and Sara
Allgood, who took it over.

Except for the heroine, the piece scarcely exists. The
English upper classes, lording it in their stately mansion
in Scarborough, express themselves almost entirely by gasps of
outrage, and the unfortunate actress who played Mrs.
Chichester for three years must surely have been close to a
nervous breakdown. Peg's sufferings among the Chichesters
are alleviated by Jerry, a personable neighbour, who drops
in from time to time wearing riding breeches or evening
dress (light summer overcoat and Homburg hat), and
urges her to make the best of things. In the last act he reveals
that her reward for having done so is to inherit five thousand
a year under the will of an uncle, and that he himself is Sir
Gerald, the local baronet, and her guardian—though why
she should need a guardian with Dad alive and kicking in
New York is not explained.

Peg, to her credit, rejects this insufferable patronage
and leaves by the garden door for America. But she is
terrified of thunder, which now conveniently breaks out
L., and rushes back into Jerry's arms. The curtain falls
on her rueful rendering of Dad's favourite quotation:
"Sure, there's nothing half so sweet in life as love's young
dream."

With this innocent and fatuous vehicle, Synge's Maurya
and Yeats's Kathleen set out to conquer the Antipodes, and
succeeded. They loved her, they went again and again to see
her; and when presently it was learned that the young man
who played Jerry was not only a real Jerry offstage, but also
the real admirer of Miss Allgood, the romantic Australian
heart was full to overflowing.

Sally's relations with colleagues at the Abbey had never
gone beyond comradeship, and it is known that she refused
several offers of marriage; one of them was from Arthur
Sinclair, who was to become Molly's second husband. At first

she did not appear very interested in Henson either. He was a good deal younger than herself, and not a Roman Catholic. A friend recalls his confiding to her his ardent wish to marry Sally, and she did not think he stood a chance; they seemed to have so little in common.

But his persistence was rewarded. They were married in a registry office in Melbourne in September of 1916, and went through a religious ceremony at the Central Methodist Mission in Sydney in the following January.

And as it turned out, she was wonderfully fortunate. Gerald Henson proved as good as he was beautiful, and independent witnesses confirm that his first thought was always for Sally's comfort and happiness. With so many virtues and graces, it would be too much to expect that he should also have been a good actor, and the general impression is that he was no more than adequate as Peg's wooer; though indeed a part so idiotic might well have baffled a Laurence Olivier. But he had a generous appreciation of his wife's genius, and was willing to subordinate his career to hers. Presumably he was not robust, since he was not in the armed forces although of military age.

With this ideal comrade by her side, her Australian sojourn was a happy one, even if it added little to her artistic stature. She made friends, visited Sydney homes and enchanted her hosts by her singing of Irish folksongs; in turn she was very ready to hear stories of the outback and meet its salty characters. And some enlightened persons recalled that she had been associated with more important work than *Peg*. The *Sydney Theatre World*, for instance, suggested "the possibility of hearing this distinguished artist in readings of some of the plays the history of which is bound up with the history of the Abbey Theatre—plays in which Miss Allgood has proved herself a character actress of rare emotional powers. I suggest readings, for the very obvious reason that it would be completely impossible to produce these plays without an Irish cast, and that could not be obtained in this country. . . . In *Riders to the Sea* we have one of her best character parts."

And a New Zealand critic, while finding that her gurgling laugh as Peg was as delicious as "the gulps made by the Malfroy geyser at Rotorua on a still moonlit night", confessed that her acting "made me yearn to be made miserable by seeing her in some of those dreary woe-stricken plays of morbid Irish life by Synge and Lady Gregory and Yeats . . . are we to see this actress in anything else but Peg? Peg is good enough for most people, and I laughed and cried at it enough, heaven knows; but at the same time I could not shut out the play's defects from my intelligence."

Nor, of course, could Sally either. She had her moments of homesickness, and wrote to Lady Gregory from Melbourne in July of 1917: "I often think of you, dear friend, and wonder how you are, and I long to be back again, but alas this terrible war will prevent my getting home for heaven knows how long as women are absolutely forbidden to leave Australia at present, in fact we can't go from Australia to New Zealand without a passport. This is a wonderful country but I long for my beloved Ireland. What is the Abbey doing lately? . . . at times I feel lost here."

She was pregnant, which may account for her depression; and at length Peg's career came to a temporary halt. On January 18th, 1918, she gave birth to a daughter, who was christened Mary, and lived only an hour. It was a bitter grief, but she was still only thirty-five, and might reasonably hope for another child.

She and Henson spent the summer making a film, *Just Peggy*, a new experience for her. "My first day in front of a camera was a worse ordeal than any first night could ever be," she told a reporter. They had bought themselves an attractive small house, "the dearest little colonial cottage" in the Sydney suburb of Mosman. She describes her rooms, her garden, her pets ("three canarys one sings divinely, a grey and pink parrot who hasn't begun to talk yet, and a white cockatoo with a pink crest"), in a lyrical letter to Sarah Purser. But it concludes, "one is at present intellectually starved here, some worthy souls are trying to form a Stage Society and put on the world's masterpieces but I feel very doubtful about its success."

The Tait contract had ended, and in the autumn Sally and Jerry began another New Zealand tour, this time for Lionel Walsh, who retains a glowing memory of Sally's professionalism under the often tough conditions of one-night stands. She took in her stride draughty ill-lit halls, inadequate dressing-rooms, sometimes nothing but a folding screen to change behind. "Sara Allgood would complain," he recalls, "the fighting Irish was there—but when the curtain went up, she was a dedicated player and gave only of her best. Sara Allgood as the complete actress took her place with the leaders. At all times, no matter how trying the day's travel, no matter how badly supported, no matter how ill-mannered country race-night audiences might be, she made her entrance without the trickery peculiar to so many actresses. She would pause, and perhaps for a fleeting moment step out of character, just a mere toss of her head or some such trivial departure from the rehearsed business, and in a flash the unruly men of the backblocks were tamed."

The tour, as it proceeded, did double the business of any Mr. Walsh had previously sent to New Zealand. Then in early November, the terrible influenza epidemic which had been raging throughout the Far East struck the Dominion, and by Government order all the theatres were closed. The company returned to Wellington, intending to take the first steamer back to Sydney. They arrived to find half the population stricken with influenza, and all succumbed themselves. Sally fell gravely ill, then Henson fatally.

He was rushed from their hotel to one of the makeshift hospitals which had been set up in church halls and school-rooms, died there, and was buried with forty-four other

victims in a trench grave. Mr. Walsh, just risen from his own
sickbed, vividly recalls the nightmare of trying to discover
what had happened to his leading man, and then of trying
to identify the grave, in order that it might later be marked
by a proper stone and inscription.

Shipping was disrupted, but with friends' help Sally
managed to get back to Sydney, early in December, by
cargo-boat. On the 5th she poured out her grief in a letter to
Lady Gregory:

> It is with a heart almost breaking that I write to tell you
> that I have just lost my dear dear husband. I know you
> will give me all your sympathy, I feel utterly lost and alone.
> We were touring round New Zealand, and in some of the
> later towns the influenza epidemic started, things got so
> bad that we finally decided to close the tour and return to
> Wellington and get the next boat back to Sydney. We
> both got ill on our arrival, went to a hotel, and couldn't
> get a doctor or nurse for love or money. We were there for
> three days before we got help, and by that time the disease
> had taken such a hold on him that he had no chance. He
> was taken off to hospital and died a week later. I am nearly
> distracted, he was so good and devoted to me, I feel utterly
> lost without him. As soon as I can arrange things I shall
> return home, and if possible I'll be back in Dublin some
> time in February. I hope I shall see you then, and have a
> little talk about the past and future.

But it was still no easier to get a passage home, and in the
event, she remained a further eighteen months in Australia,
finding much kindness and sympathy in her bereavement.
Tait's gave her another contract and a generous retaining fee
until the theatres could re-open (for the influenza had closed
Australian theatres also). A new leading man, Lawrence
Cecil, was brought out from England and a company was
re-formed to give *Peg* and two further plays, a dramatisation
of H. A. Vachell's *Quinneys*, and an American piece called
Old Lady 31. Neither would seem to have had much merit,

but they did at least spare Sally from having to play any more ingénues.

"She was a brilliant actress," writes Mr. Cecil, who has remained in Australia, "and her Peg was magnificent— infinitely superior in my opinion to the original, Laurette Taylor, whom I saw in America. Sally's infectious, musical, delightful, impish laugh was something never to be forgotten." There could hardly be a better tribute to Sally's professionalism than that this was the impression she made on a colleague, at a time when her personal happiness had crashed in ruins.

But she was profoundly affected by the disaster. She had always been a practising Catholic, but now she saw the deaths of her child and of her husband as a judgment upon her for having married a Protestant, and religious observance became expiation as well as relief. She never spoke of those she had lost, and only her intimate friends knew the history of her short married life, or why it was that, though not normally a woman to meddle in other people's affairs, any suggestion of neglect or risk to a baby would drive her nearly frantic.

Most people in Ireland are still unaware that she was ever married. Even a producer for whom she did an important season's work commented to me that the intensely maternal quality of her acting was mysterious in one who had never been wife or mother. He looked astonished when I was able to tell him: "But she was."

At last, in July of 1920, she came home—to an England officially at peace, but to an Ireland still very much at war.

10

It is generally believed in Ireland that both Molly's marriages were failures, but the statement is not an accurate description of the first, a union in which the partners, through many stresses and enforced separations, remained in love up to the end.

G. H. Mair was to Molly a patient and devoted husband. He did not repeat Synge's mistake of trying to mould her, but accepted her as she was, and when he needed intellectual companionship, looked for it elsewhere. And in return she loved him as much, probably, as she was capable of loving anyone; but that she proved "a lucky wife" can hardly be maintained.

Mair was not a genius like Synge, but he was a highly gifted and sensitive person, equally brilliant as a journalist and in the mysterious and often dangerous secret service work he did for the Foreign Office during the war. When war ended, he headed the Press Section of the British peace delegation, and is credited with working thirty-six hours at a stretch to summarise the text of the Versailles Treaty. But he was highly-strung and febrile, sharing some of Molly's weaknesses but not her underlying Allgood toughness; hospitable, generous to a fault, a burner of the candle at both ends. His fluent vocabulary was, as a colleague wrote after his death, "defective in the one respect that it did not contain a single No. . . . Lovable in his errors and weak even in his power, Mair gave more than he ever received." He should have married a woman who would have been a calming and steadying influence, not a quicksilver Pegeen Mike. In some ways perhaps he *was* Christy Mahon—is not genius apt to be prophetic? But Christy, it will be remembered, contrives to escape from Pegeen.

If Mair burned himself out at thirty-eight with his great promise largely unfulfilled, it was to some extent Molly's fault. But to blame her would be as futile as to scold the west wind for bringing rain. Actresses of uncommon fascination and talent are seldom remarkable for the sober domestic virtues, and this has never prevented clever and imaginative men from ardently desiring to marry them.

She bore him two children, a girl, Pegeen, and a boy, John Dunbar; and if she rushed back to the stage as soon as her confinements were ended, it was not from any discontent with married life but because the stage was in her blood. She was with the Liverpool Repertory Company for a season; then with Tree in Shakespeare in London; and constantly with J. B. Fagan, that staunch supporter of the new Irish drama on the London stage. Her two eldest brothers, Harry and the beloved George, were killed within weeks of each other in 1915, and George's death hit her very hard. It was from this time that her serious drinking began.

She was back at the Abbey in 1916 to create the part of Aunt Helen in Lennox Robinson's *The Whiteheaded Boy*, one of the few Abbey plays of that period to take the English public's fancy; it was to prove a useful vehicle for both Allgoods in years to come. In 1916 she played old Mary in *The Tinker's Wedding* in London; this is the Synge comedy which could not be put on in Ireland because it made game of a priest. If I could choose, I would almost rather have seen her rollicking, raucous, pathetic Mary than her Pegeen. She must have been the old reprobate to the life.

She had leads in the Abbey's first complete Shaw season, in 1917, but after that it saw her no more. She needed bigger money than it could afford. Both she and Mair earned handsome salaries, but they lived on a scale that swallowed every penny, keeping open house in Chelsea for the world of letters and art.

When Sally returned to London in June of 1920 the theatre which had nurtured them both was going through its grimmest ordeal, with Dublin in the grip of the Black and Tan war, curfew and the threat of ambush reducing audiences to a plucky handful. And Sally too, though she found a letter of welcome from Lady Gregory, realised that for the time being she would do better to stay where she was.

Sally to Lady Gregory, June 4th, 1920:

Oh I do thank you for your dear dear letter to me, my exile was worth it for your sweet welcome. I shall be in London for a while longer. . . . Bernard Fagan has approached me to play in the Whiteheaded Boy, which is due to open I believe about the end of September, but we're still at loggerheads over the question of salary. So I don't really know what I'll be doing, but oh wouldn't I just love to be back in the Abbey once more. . . . All my love to you always, you splendid, brave, wonderful lady. God bless you is always the prayer of your Sally.

The same to the same, November 30th, 1920.

. . . I can't tell you how my heart bleeds for you to be in the midst of such terrible happenings. I hope you are keeping in good health and that the nervous strain isn't taking too much out of you. I have written to J. B. Fagan asking him to release me at the end of the London season, which will be about the end of January. May I hope that you will have me back at the Abbey then? I don't want a huge salary, and I'm simply aching to be back, to teach and produce in conjunction with Robinson and Dolan. I feel certain we can get them to work splendidly, and it would be a great thing to get the acting back to its old level.

Whether she would have found this attitude of slight patronage acceptable to those who had held the fort in her absence is questionable. As it turned out, the imposition of an eight o'clock curfew closed the Abbey altogether, and brought it to the verge of ruin. It was only saved by English well-wishers. Yeats and Lady Gregory launched a heroic appeal, with a series of lectures and recitals given in Fagan's Chelsea drawing-room. Sally and Molly took their old parts in *Gaol Gate*, and proved to a crowded audience that their tragic powers had deepened with the years. The money to stave off imminent bankruptcy was subscribed.

But the future of Sally and Molly, and the future of the Abbey itself, hung on more than mere finance; it hung on fresh plays. They needed a new dramatist of the first rank, and they needed him very badly indeed.

I I

If Sean O'Casey appeared at the right time for Sara Allgood, the converse is also true. He found for his greatest woman's part an interpreter who had herself been matured by a personal tragedy, now sufficiently distant to have lost its rawness and be transmutable into the material of art.

His first play, *Shadow of a Gunman*, was put on at the Abbey in the spring of 1923, and she returned to the company in the autumn—not without a certain heartburning on the part of several excellent actresses who had carried it through the years of world war and civil war in her absence. But Yeats and Lady Gregory were determined to have her back, and when *Riders* was revived, it was obvious that she was without a rival. Gabriel Fallon, who played Bartley, recalls the extraordinary sensation of hearing her speak the great dirge over his "drowned" body. He swears that he could feel the sea washing over him.

A talent of this magnitude constituted a challenge, as Yeats noted in a tribute he paid her in the *Irish Times* of January 19th, 1924:

Miss Sara Allgood is a great folk-actress. As so often
happens with a great actor or actress, she rose into fame
with a school of drama. She was born to play the old
woman in *The Well of the Saints*, and to give their first
vogue to Lady Gregory's little comedies. It is impossible
for those of us who are connected with the Abbey management to forget that night in December 1904, when for the
first time she rushed among the stage crowd in *Spreading the
News*, calling out "Give me back my man!" We never
knew until that moment that we had, not only a great
actress, but that rarest of all things, a woman comedian;
for stage humour is almost a male prerogative.

It has been more difficult in recent years to supply her
with adequate parts, for Dublin is a little tired of its admirable folk-arts, political events having turned our minds
elsewhere. Perhaps the Spaniard, Sierra, who in his plays
expounds a psychological and modern purpose through
sharply defined characters, themselves as little psychological and modern as Mrs. Broderick herself, may give her
the opportunity she needs. I am looking forward with great
curiosity to seeing her in his *Two Shepherds*, which is just
now going into rehearsal, and one of our Irish dramatists,
Mr. Casey [*sic*], has in his new play, *Juno and the Paycock*,
given her an excellent part.

Miss Allgood is no end of a problem, and the sooner our
dramatists get that into their heads and write for her the
better for them and us. If we knew how to appreciate our
geniuses, they would not have wasted her so scandalously.

In harping on her Mrs. Broderick, Yeats was wide of the
mark, for she had lost the comic touch; it is generally
admitted that her comedy in the latter half of her career was
heavy and bumbling. But her astonishing gain in tragic
power was more than compensation, as the audience
acknowledged on that legendary first night of *Juno and the
Paycock*, when the players were recalled so often that in the
end the exhausted stage-hands left the curtain up for good.
Her speaking of Juno's final prayer, "Mother of Jesus, put

away from us this murderous hatred and give us thine own eternal love", transcended folk-art and the Dublin slums and even Ireland, just as her speaking of Maurya's dirge had done, and seemed to embody a universal cry. But almost more impressive, according to Gabriel Fallon, because independent of words, was her entrance in Act 3, after the guffawing scene between Joxer and Boyle had left the audience ready to titter at whatever might come next:

"It is no exaggeration," he writes, "to say that her appearance literally *compelled* the audience to a frozen silence and held it there. Not a word was spoken by her. She did not even sigh. Her movements were few; she made no gesture. She simply opened the door, came in and sat down; and as she did so, tragedy sat at the elbow of every member of the audience." She had never forgotten that basic Fay tenet, to be sparing of movement and make every movement tell.

The Abbey was a repertory theatre, and even a big success could not be extended beyond two or three weeks. The company moved on to other plays, at least two of them with good parts for Sally: Ellen in T. C. Murray's best play, *Autumn Fires*, and Nannie in the O'Casey one-acter, *Nannie's Night Out*. But a winner like *Juno* was obviously going to do well in London; Fagan called, and presently the Abbey was again without its leading lady.

Meanwhile, O'Casey had a new play on the stocks, with a part in it designed especially for her. She confidently expected that the Abbey would postpone their first production of *The Plough and the Stars* till the London run of *Juno* should be over, and was correspondingly indignant when she found that they were not prepared to wait. Actress-like, she wished to have her cake and eat it. She writes on November 5th, 1925, to Gabriel Fallon, who had become her principal friend among the Abbey actors:

Royal Theatre, Dean Street.
I'm heartbroken about Sean's play. Oh I could lash myself for ever, praying for Juno and missing this chance of

Bessie B., but as I've said to Sean, if the Abbey thought anything of my quality as an actress surely they'd have waited at least to see if Juno caught on, and then if it did, to say Well Sally we can't wait any longer. Oh God I feel heartbroken and more sorry than I can say, but after all it really is Lennox's fault, he could have refused to let Fagan have Juno and then I'd have been back, but L. R. is a great friend of J. B. F.'s and so naturally any influence he had with the Directors he used. . . . I wonder if you know that before I got this offer, I asked the Theatre for a loan and offered to pay it back at so much per week, and also to sign a contract to stay with them for two years; why won't they realise that I'm an asset to them and keep me? Ah well, I suppose God knows why they won't, and He won't tell. . . . God bless you, let's have a line to say how "The Plough" goes, altho' I'll hate reading it, but still it will be another scourge for me.

Juno and the Paycock opened at the Royalty at the end of November, with a largely ex-Abbey cast, Molly as Mrs. Madigan and Arthur Sinclair as the Paycock; and Sally was able to report triumphantly to Fallon:

I can't tell you how happy and proud I am at the success of Juno, for the sake of the Abbey, Sean, and also myself. I had a bit of a battle, I'll tell you someday, but the result has been a glorious victory. I'm only sorry that my comrades in the Abbey weren't with me sharing it all. I'm longing to be back, now that I've "shown them" here. I've no idea how long Juno will run, but if we all get rich, what matter.

G. H. Mair, Molly's husband, died on January 3rd, 1926. Sally tells Fallon:

Poor G. H.'s death came as a dreadful shock to us all, and he was so well on Xmas Day, he had dinner with us and then went back to the nursing home, apparently quite well. Poor Molly was practically stunned with the shock of it all, and practically all the business of arranging things and seeing after things fell on me, then on top of that I had nine performances of Juno, that week and the following week. . . . I heard the other day that Sean is getting rather a swelled head, he was very haughty with Fagan over the rights of the "Plough", and he Sean said to J. B. that his offer was as much use to him as a half lettuce to a starving man, that is a funny thing to say isn't it? Oh I do hope Sean isn't going to become "difficult", its one fault I have to find with the majority of Irish people the minute they have a little success, it seems to go straight to their heads, I did think Sean was different. . . . Do tell me your frank opinion of the "Plough".

The Plough and the Stars was presented to a restive and finally rioting audience at the Abbey on February 8th, 1926, with Maureen Delany, who had only hitherto been considered suited to comic parts, giving a moving performance as Bessie Burgess, the role that should have been Sally's. Sally's letter to Fallon commiserating with the company on their ordeal has a faint whiff of sour grapes:

It must have been a terrible week for you all, what a pity Sean didn't go up on to the stage and give it back to them in their own vernacular, that his play was the "truth", and that they could b——y well take it or leave it, that would have been the thing to do. I have just read the Plough and I confess I'm disappointed, I think Mrs. Gogan the best character part in the whole play, and honestly from the reading I don't think it can compare with Juno for beauty, humanity and wonderful faith and that's what's so badly needed today. Faith, especially, in a Divine Providence, that's to my mind the wonderful lesson Juno teaches, and why I adore it so much. Our audiences are beginning to get smaller, but their applause and enthusiasm are, if possible, greater than before. Yesterday, after the matinee, they stood up and cheered me.

Plough was given in London later in the year, with Sally at last playing the Protestant virago, Bessie Burgess, who dies a heroine's death. It is a much shorter part than Juno, but in the right hands effective, and in Sally's it was unforgettable. The Fluther Good was Arthur Sinclair, who by this time was Molly's second husband.

He had been her admirer for years, and must often, it is to be feared, have been a trial to poor Mair. She married him within six months of Mair's death, a move bitterly resented by her children, and one not calculated to promote a more regular way of life. The marriage almost at once ran into squalls. But whatever Sinclair's shortcomings as a husband, he was an admirable actor. As the Paycock, and as Fluther Good, he was considered by many to excel Barry Fitzgerald, who had created the parts at the Abbey.

Molly's talents had veered in the opposite direction to Sally's, becoming more broadly comic. She could be brilliantly, wickedly funny, particularly as a mimic, and she could be deeply pathetic, but real tragedy was out of her range. She did ultimately play Juno, and made of her a very recognisable Dublin slum-character; she wisely did not attempt the awe-inspiring saintliness with which Sally invested the part.

O'Casey's two masterpieces kept the three of them in constant work. They toured America in 1927, and again the following year. Sally had been in two minds about the engagement; more trouble was predicted with *Plough*, "and honestly, dear," she wrote to Lady Gregory, "I don't feel I can bear another *Playboy* riot. O'Casey is a clever man but he hasn't Synge's greatness and I don't feel why I should fight for his play."

But the worst they had to endure was a whispering campaign against *Plough*, which at first kept audiences away. Sinclair put on *Juno* instead, and they came crowding back. "Sally fairly stunned them," Tony Quinn, who was a member of the company on both tours, recalls. He also remembers that there was seldom a time when the leading man and the two leading ladies were all three on speaking terms; but in spite of, or perhaps because of, this electric atmosphere, they gave superb performances. For many American playgoers, this was the new Irish drama's finest hour.

Sally had become a passionate card-player. The Atlantic crossings were whiled away with bridge sessions, and in the States the stage-hands, among whom she was always popular, taught her to play poker. The short part of Bessie gave her a lot of time off-stage, and it was marvellous to watch her reduce an audience to tears with that tremendous death-scene, and then scamper back to resume her place in the game. It was, however, fatal to let Molly join her at the bridge table. The very real affection, spiced with professional rivalry, which bound the sisters could survive all strains except Molly's refusal to treat bridge as anything but a lark.

In between tours and London engagements, Sally would return for short refresher-courses at the Abbey. She was always sure of a welcome from Lady Gregory and from the Dublin audience, but with the rest of the team she was not so popular. "Sally uses the Abbey when it suits her," Lennox Robinson would grumble, and of course it was true. Some London manager would telephone with a lucrative offer, and off she would go. It was not her fault; she needed her panoply of success, her picture hats and silver-fox furs and velvet dresses; she was chronically short of money, and though she got twice the salary of the regular players, it was still only a fraction of what she could command in the West End or in America.

The Abbey had always had to face this problem when one of its children attained wider fame; it still does. Lady Gregory noted wistfully in her journal: "Once they get our actors over there, as Sally, they don't let them go. I think I must write an epilogue about old, old men and women tottering in to a half-forgotten scene, to be ready for them when they do come back at last!"

But it was not all roses and stardom for those who left. Sally was a world name, "the great Irish actress"; she had now to take a further step and become "the great actress" *tout court*. She had, that is to say, to make the transition from a native to an international drama. It was a transition she never quite achieved.

12

Her nearest approach to it was when she played a Dublin season with Hilton Edwards's Gate Theatre company. With Lady Gregory's death in 1932 she lost her principal Abbey champion; Lennox Robinson never ceased to pay tribute to her in print, but he was no longer willing to have her use the Abbey as her port in a storm, and succeeded in convincing Yeats that she was no longer a draw. Hilton Edwards and Micheal MacLiammoir thought otherwise. They knew that Dublin loved her still, and they believed that she had a great deal more to offer Dublin, if she could get away from what seemed to them the rather limiting Abbey tradition.

Her parts were Madame Raquin in *Thérèse Raquin*, Madame Ranevskaya in *The Cherry Orchard*, and Millamant in *The Way of the World*. From Mr. Edwards, an Englishman wedded to the cause of drama in Ireland, one gets an interestingly dispassionate view of her art.

"Unexcelled on her own ground," he says. "As good as Edith Evans when a part suited her, but she hadn't Evans's range. Her Mme Raquin was terrifying and tremendous, the best I've seen—it's essentially a peasant character. Her Ranevskaya didn't sufficiently suggest the aristocrat, but it was earthy and interesting, you certainly felt the attachment to the soil. She made a brave attempt at Millamant, but it was hopeless." He goes on to suggest that this is a limitation common to Abbey actors; that they are a national as much as a dramatic movement, drawing their strength from the soil and history of their country. They do not get sufficient experience of parts outside the Abbey range, and when they leave the Abbey they are lost. They are not really suited to the international stage.

This, of course, is a rival producer's view, and it will be hotly disputed by Abbey supporters. But whether or no it is applicable today, there was a good deal of truth in it in the 1930's. An unconscious snobbery still demanded that the big tragic parts should be played in upper-middle-class English accents; a north-country Hamlet would be unthinkable; an Irish Lear was strictly for the Abbey.

The attitude has largely altered, but the change came too late for Sally and Molly. O'Casey was one of those who blazed the trail for a whole new school of proletarian dramatists. Not only are there now many more parts suited to a Sara Allgood, but there is a new approach to roles in which she might have excelled had she been given the chance.

Mr. Edwards himself acknowledges as much when he concludes: "She had the possibilities of a great classic actress. We ought to have done more with her, found her parts into which the question of social class doesn't enter. I've always regretted that we didn't play her as Hecuba. She'd have been wonderful—Paxinou's quality."

One thinks of *Mother Courage*, too, she should certainly have done that.

13

She made a talking film of *Juno*, an English film in which her acting won the highest praise, but the Irishness of others in the cast left a good deal to be desired. 1940 found her again playing Juno in New York, and hearing the siren call of Hollywood. Barry Fitzgerald was making a fortune there, Una O'Connor was continually busy in supporting roles, and why not she? So to Hollywood she went, and in 1945 took American citizenship; and Dublin heard impressive stories of her fine house and lavish way of living now that she was "a famous film star". Alas, it was a good way from the truth.

Hollywood had not the faintest notion of how to use her; all she got were "quaint old Irishwoman" bit-parts, cooks, landladies or barmaids. She was slightly more in evidence in *Lady Hamilton* and in *How Green Was My Valley*, but never in any way extended. It was not altogether Hollywood's fault. Fitzgerald and O'Connor, for all the fame they achieved, were essentially supporting players and could tuck in cosily anywhere. Sally was in quite another class, and when put to do unimportant work she called too much attention to herself, or showed up the shoddiness of the film, or threw it out of gear.

She did make some money at last, and sensibly invested it in a fine house; then there were long spells without work, and she was glad to rent the house and move into cheap lodgings. She always kept up a brave front in her letters to the family (though she grew desperately lonely, and would sometimes telephone her niece Pegeen in London, just to hear a familiar voice). But in her letters to Gabriel Fallon she is honest about her failure, though never quite without hope that her luck will change.

On October 18th, 1947, she tells him of her determination to "break the vicious circle which seems to have surrounded me all this year, I am trying hard to keep my chin up, but it becomes rather a strain after awhile, the old neck and back get tired. . . . I hear you are on rather good terms with Gabriel Pascal, would you mention my name to him sometime in the course of conversation?—it would be a great boost to my career if I was asked to go to Dublin to make a film with him. . . . I hate being inactive, and I have still hopes that I will make some more 'career' before I die. Have you read Mary Colum's *Life and the Dream*? So many books have come out this year, by different people, and I am mentioned in them, that I am getting frightened, I feel as though I were reading my own obituary notices."

In July of next year she complains about her bad back, a legacy of rheumatic fever when she was a child: "this will explain the reason of my being in the deeps of depression, then the work situation here is pretty grim, thank God I at least have the house, which, now that I'm starting to rent it, gives me a small monthly income, so that on that side I really have quite a lot to be thankful for." She is taking a Summer Theatre job: "they just pay the minimum salary, but it makes a lovely change and holiday, I do Juno at Ogunquit, a fashionable summer resort . . . there is a slight nibble going on in New York for me for the fall."

In March of 1949 she made over to Fallon, as her closest remaining Abbey friend, her five shares in the theatre. "In the early days of the Abbey, the Directors God rest them decided to give certain actors shares in the theatre, I was among the few who got them, Frank Fay was one, W. G. another, Padraic Colum another. There is no value of any sort attached to them, except the honour and glory, oh there is something, I believe if they wanted to sell or dispose of the

Abbey, the shareholders would have to be consulted and would be entitled to a share of the sale."

In September she has changed her address. "Strictly entre nous I have been very worried financially and these movings were to try and find cheaper places to live, a pretty serious problem, for the love of God don't tell Joan [her sister] it would break her heart, then all the expense I've been under trying to get relief from this blasted neuritis, and plus no jobs I've had a pretty tough time. . . . I may do a revival of the Whiteheaded Boy at a little theatre here, just to keep in circulation, they pay nothing, but it's activity of a sort."

Next month she lands a small part in the film *Cheaper by the Dozen*, "the salary is cut to the bone but no matter, it's activity, and that's the main thing".

In December she acknowledges a magazine he had sent her with pictures of Molly in her last film, *Saints and Sinners*, and tributes to them both. "My poor Molly, how terribly changed, the poor darling certainly looks the Mother of Sorrows. God bless and help her, I hear she is not so well. Your tribute to me warmed my sad heart, and I am so honoured that you should put me in the same category as Duse, never shall I forget when we did Juno in London, when Margot Asquith hailed me at a party in her house as 'the Irish Duse', it was a wonderful tribute, but I must thank Sean O'Casey for all that. . . . I am now timidly stepping into Television, and between ourselves I hate the medium, it's really a bastard art, oh one can't possibly call it an art. . . ."

Television occupied her last working months, still not much to her satisfaction. January 12th, 1950: "I am gently creeping into Television, its frightful but it's a little activity, they pay nothing according to American standards, 50 dollars a week but it will improve I hope. Alan Mowbray is the guest star along with myself, I am praise be allowed to sing a little, a thing they would never let me do in films, so that part is a small pleasure, but I feel like an imbecile being directed by a robot camera, it's a strange turn the 'arts' are taking, that is if by any stretch of imagination one can call TV an ART."

She died in Hollywood after a heart attack, on September 13th, 1950.

14

Molly's last twenty years were a formidable rake's progress —divorce, drink, poverty, constant frantic appeals to Synge's trustees for advances on the small annual income he had left her. Yet it would be misleading to call her story tragic. She was a naturally gay soul, and contrived to get a large amount of fun out of her worst predicaments. The only thing she really dreaded was boredom, and that she somehow always managed to avoid.

She also, astonishingly in view of the drinking and unreliability, contrived to be almost always in work. She was more versatile and adaptable than Sally, a better mimic, less obviously a star. Producers had an affection for her. If the script of play, film or radio called for a battling Irish termagent, or a shawlie mother on a pitiful deathbed, it was of Maire O'Neill that everyone thought first. Give her half a chance and she could still bring the house down. She was billed to broadcast in a radio version of O'Casey's *Silver Tassie* when she died.

She had once been a handful to her mother and grandmother; now she was a handful to her children, particularly when out of work. She had a habit then of sweeping into expensive restaurants, announcing "I am the great Irish actress" and demanding the best table, while they un-

willingly followed her, not knowing where to look. Her son
John, a promising young writer, was killed in 1942 while
training to fly with the R.A.F.

At the end she appears to have had some kind of seizure.
She was found lying in the fireplace with her hair charred,
and died a week later in hospital, on November 2nd, 1952.

Lennox Robinson, who had worked so long with the sisters,
and been enchanted and exasperated by them both, was
moved to quote in his appreciation of Molly Nashe's lovely
elegy for beauty:

> Brightness falls from the air,
> Queens have died young and fair,
> Dust hath closed Helen's eye.

It was not literally applicable. They had not died young
and fair, but old and in a sense defeated, and the defeat had
been in some part due to their own failings. But in their
heyday they had interpreted and inspired a dramatic movement which was one of youth, poetry and revolt. That was
how he remembered them, and so did thousands more.

And no one who remembers them is willing to admit that
their talents have been equalled since, though a distinguished
new generation of Irish actors had arisen, and some find
echoes of Sally in Siobhan McKenna, and of Molly in
Eithne Dunne. The great roles of the Irish drama can stand
independently of the interpreter, and are a lasting challenge,
which each generation will, no doubt, interpret in a different
way.

But to those who saw Sally and Molly play them, they can
never be quite as good again.

SOURCES:

Lady Gregory: *Our Irish Theatre*. New York, Putnam, 1914.
—— *Journals, 1916–1930*, edited by Lennox Robinson, London, Putnam, 1946.
Lennox Robinson: *Ireland's Abbey Theatre*. London, Sidgwick & Jackson, 1951.
W. G. Fay and Catherine Carswell: *The Fays of the Abbey Theatre*. London, Rich & Cowan, 1935.
David H. Greene and Edward M. Stephens: *J. M. Synge*. New York, Macmillan, 1959.
Micheal MacLiammoir: *All for Hecuba*. London, Methuen, 1946.
Maire nic Shiubhlaigh: *The Splendid Years*. Dublin, Duffy, 1955.

Henderson Scrapbook of the Abbey Theatre, National Library of Ireland.
Unpublished letters and poems of J. M. Synge to Molly Allgood (by permission of the Synge Trustees).
Unpublished MSS. of Lady Gregory (by permission of Major Richard Gregory).
Unpublished letters of Frank and Willie Fay to Lady Gregory (by permission of Mr. Gerard Fay).

Recollections of Miss Pegeen Mair, Mr. Bill Allgood, Mrs. E. M. Stephens, the late Miss Maureen Delany, Mr. Gabriel Fallon, Mr. Tony Quinn, Mr. Hilton Edwards.

Information on Sara Allgood's Australian years, supplied by readers of the *Sydney Morning Herald*: Mme Celia Arcana, Mr. Lawrence H. Cecil, Mr. Roy Channel, Mrs. D. E. Cooke, Mrs. A. E. H. Grey, Mr. Walter Linton, Miss D. E. R. Mason, Mrs. B. M. McDonald, Mr. Ray Vaughan, Mr. Lionel Walsh.

ENVOI

DUBLIN is a city richly inhabited by ghosts, both because the national temperament preserves the mannerisms of the dead in anecdote and folklore, even if the precise nature of their achievements grows hazy; and also because the city has lost, as yet, so little of the physical charm they knew. One can still look down a rose-red Georgian street to a blue barrier of mountains, and experience that lifting of the spirits that has ravished poets and patriots for two hundred years. Native or stranger, we all surrender.

Each of us, naturally, tends to see the ghosts that concern us most, and to me as I pursued my five heroines from one old friend to another—invariably to be received with a sympathy and vividness of recollection which I cannot hope to have reproduced—it often seemed that the whisk of their skirts had barely preceded me round the street-corner.

Two Maud Gonnes dodge each other disconcertingly up and down O'Connell Street: the young goddess, triumphant on her outside car and guarded by her Great Dane, and the black-draped sibyl, leading her procession of militant women to some protest meeting on "the ruins corner". But O'Connell Street and Bridge it has to be. No other setting, even in spacious Dublin, is grandiose enough for that six foot of female splendour. Sometimes the faithful Willie hovers behind her, but not often. The ghost of Yeats is less and less easily surprised in Dublin. Perhaps it is the penalty for belonging now to the whole world.

Constance, of course, must be sought on Stephens Green. Her dark-green jacket, her slouch hat with the cock feathers, the glint of her rifle are camouflaged among the trees round the little lake; but at any moment she may emerge, sweep aside the lunchtime strollers and the irrelevant statue among the flower-beds, and order the digging of a trench. Westland Row station, too, sees her arriving, pale and radiant after English imprisonment, to greet the adoring crowds; she opens her arms in love, for victory lies ahead; beyond victory lies disillusion, but that she can't know.

There is a second Constance, the artist from the Mayo shore. You find her in one of those hanging valleys, high up on the Dublin mountains, from which the city shines far off like some distant Jerusalem. She is making a sketch, not a very good one, but that does not matter. It is important to her to take beauty through her pencil into her heart and mind, so that she may have it with her next time they shut her up in prison.

It is no good calling on Sarah Purser at Mespil House, for it has vanished, staircase, plaster ceiling, park, lake and all. Utilitarian blocks of red-brick flats cover its site. But she pauses for a moment outside her old house in Harcourt Terrace, immensely busy but not too busy to note the Monet-like effect of light on the canal. She constantly supervises progress at the two great galleries, doing a little ghostly scolding now and again, no doubt, but gratified on the whole with what she finds: half the Lane Pictures restored to the Municipal, and her Friends still making their contributions, while at the National the funds accruing from Bernard Shaw's legacy enable her colleague Thomas MacGreevy and his successor James White to acquire Old Masters even in the fiercely competitive markets of today.

But most strongly is her presence to be felt at the Tower of Glass. There it still is, the ramshackle backyard workshop; a gifted young stained-glass artist, Patrick Pollen, acquired it from the heirs of Kitty O'Brien, the last working survivor of her band. He is carrying on, in a contemporary idiom of which she would entirely approve, the tradition of Healy and Hone, and he and his staff are as busy as the Tower was in her heyday. Among their many commissions are the windows for the new cathedral in Galway.

Sally in her maturity at the Abbey speaks through every Bessie Burgess, every Kathleen ni Houlihan, every Juno; even in reaction against her interpretations, no actress can ignore them. But it was easier to picture her in the flesh in the old Abbey, peeling, battered, pock-marked with fire, but still extraordinarily powerful in atmosphere, which has been swept away to make room for the new one.

The mature Molly belongs to London. Her Dublin ghost is a young girl, coming away from Harcourt Street station, itself a ghost because the line which ran from it to Bray and the Wicklow Hills died long ago. Her face is set with the strain and effort of meeting a great and dying man's demanding love. She will be late for rehearsal, and cheeky when she is reprimanded; and she will then shrug off every preoccupation, and give such a performance, whether as golden girl or as cackling crone, that even Willie Fay momentarily forgives her.

Five passionate, wilful, self-forgetting ghosts; happy because absorbed, through no matter what setback and difficulty, by work which in one form or another will redound to the glory of Ireland.

The creatures have a purpose, and their eyes are bright with it.

INDEX